Acknowledgements

This project report is a result of CIRIA research project RP644 Sustainable Construction Targets & Indicators. The project was funded by the participating organisations, CIRIA's Core programme and the DTI through its Partners in Innovation scheme.

CIRIA would like to thank members of the project steering group for their significant contributions throughout the project. The steering group comprised:

Steve Priddy	Arup
Barrie Mould	Atkins
Martin Brock	Balfour Beatty Civil Engineering Limited
Andrew Cripps	Buro Happold
Doug Janikiewicz	Carillion
Paul Donnelly	Laing plc
James Wishart	MWH
Neil Moore	Skanska
Steve Hunt	Taylor Woodrow Construction
Charlotte Whitmore	WSP
Bruce Sharpe	Forum for the Future
David Graham	Royal Bank of Scotland
Mervyn Jones	Davis Langdon Consultancy (DTI agent)

CIRIA's project manager for the project was Jeff Kersey. The project director was Dr Owen Jenkins. Dr Alistair Bird of AEAT assisted in a number of workshops and in preparing related briefings papers.

Executive summary

Introduction

Despite intensive development of industry KPIs, practical understanding of their implementation is in its infancy. To help address this the project set out to engage in the practical trialling of CIRIA's sustainable construction key performance indicators, and to distil the key lessons learned for dissemination to the wider industry.

Focusing on CIRIA's environmental and social indicators, the approach involved bringing together 10 major companies who demonstrated a strong willingness to exchange ideas and to share detailed information from their extensive experiences.

Although experience during the project indicated that no standard set of detailed sustainability KPIs was likely to be adopted by the industry as a whole, the CIRIA suite of indicators was found to be a suitable source of indicators for supporting the achievement of organisational targets to improve performance. Reflecting variety in company type and the construction projects they undertook, formal benchmarking between companies remained largely aspirational at the time of the project.

Driving the need to participate in the Club were factors such the desire to engage with the sustainability concept and to understand the benefits of reporting and comparing achievements with peers (formally or informally). Some companies were interested in developing high profile sustainability strategies. Most companies wanted to assess the opportunities from integrating different management systems and to find ways to maximise impacts from existing internal initiatives and best practice.

A range of factors was considered in deciding which indicators to implement. Companies considered how particular indicators would relate to organisational aims, core values and stakeholder concerns. Other considerations were how they supported preventative action and the assessment of continual improvement and trends. Companies also thought about how the new indicators would complement existing indicators and whether they dealt with the priority concerns for the organisation. Inter-project benchmarking was also discussed.

Data availability and management were key topics of discussion throughout the project. Companies found that much relevant data flowed through their organisations, but it was often in forms not suitable for the chosen indicators. The companies discussed various strategies for identifying, adapting, collecting, managing and reporting data. These addressed resource implications, adaption of existing management systems, personnel requirements and other issues.

As companies moved towards the adoption of particular sets of indicators, discussions on their nature and role became quite detailed. This reflected the complexity of the management task around implementing sustainable construction practices. Discussions covered a range of topics such as the need for a project cut-off size to avoid overburdening smaller projects; whether there was clarity on the interpretation of the indicators' parameters and whether the normalisation measure was appropriate to the circumstances the indicator would be applied to. Companies also discussed issues of consistency of definitions and regularity of reporting between operating businesses and the extent of company responsibilities and control over supply chain activities.

LONDON 2004

Sustainable construction – implementing targets and indicators

Experiences from CIRIA's Pioneers' Club

J R Kersey

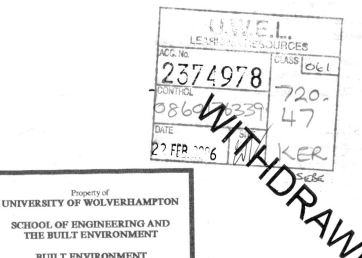

CIRIA *sharing knowledge ■ building best practice*

CIRIA, Classic House, 174-180 Old Street, London EC1V 9BP, UK.
Telephone: +44 (0)20 7549 3300   Fax: +44 (0)20 7253 0523
Email: enquiries@ciria.org   Web: www.ciria.org

Summary

A key performance indicator (KPI) measures the performance of an activity that is important to the success of a company. The indicator's role is to enable the recording of progress towards pre-set achievable targets for that activity.

Despite intensive development of industry KPIs, practical understanding of their implementation is in its infancy. This book describes the trialling of a set of KPIs for sustainable construction and distills the lessons learned to enable their dissemination to the wider industry.

The approach involved the formation of a club of 10 major companies that demonstrated a strong willingness to exchange ideas and to share detailed information from their extensive experiences. Its goal was to understand from a practical perspective the role of indicators in driving the participating companies, and the industry in general, towards the reporting of real performance improvement against a standard set of clearly defined sustainability criteria.

Sustainable construction – implementing targets and indicators.
Experiences from CIRIA's Pioneers' Club

Kersey, J R

CIRIA C633   © CIRIA 2004   RP644   ISBN 0-86017-633-9

Keywords
Sustainable construction, supply chain management, benchmarking, key performance indicators, KPIs, project management, environmental good practice, health and safety, sustainable resource use, pollution prevention, waste minimisation.

Reader interest	Classification	
Directors	AVAILABILITY	Unrestricted
	CONTENT	Guide
Health and safety managers	STATUS	Committee-guided
Environmental managers		
Supply chain and procurement	USER	Directors
managers		Health and safety managers
Public relations managers		Environmental managers
		Supply chain and procurement
		managers
		Public relations managers

Published by CIRIA, Classic House, 174-180 Old Street, London EC1V 9BP, UK

British Library Cataloguing in Publication Data
A catalogue record is available for this book from the British Library

In implementing indicators the companies considered the requirements for trialling and periodic review, and assessed the benefits of limiting the initial applicability of the indicators to selected parts of the business. They also assessed software requirements, quality control and the need to achieve buy-in from data collectors and senior management.

Companies also considered whether existing knowledge sharing, awareness raising and training approaches could be adapted to support sustainability strategies and related indicators implementation. Sustainability training was also addressed.

Contents

1 Background

1.1 Introduction

The sustainability agenda

The goal for the Pioneers' Club was to understand, from the practical perspective, the role of indicators in driving the participating companies and the industry in general, towards the reporting of real performance improvement against a standard set of clearly defined sustainability criteria.

Although a challenging idea for business, an increasing number of major companies now see sustainability as a potential route for business advantage. As a conceptual framework it can provide potential benefits from a balanced understanding of company impacts and responsibilities, and the key emerging pressures from important stakeholders including the public.

The scale of the concept, and the associated changing demands being made of the industry, mean that companies are faced with complex decision-making. In the absence of established route maps for the way forward the sector's approach is fragmented, with different companies dealing with different priority issues in different ways.

The Pioneers' Club has grown out of this situation and is part of CIRIA's on-going response to the industry's need for guidance on establishing sustainable construction practices.

Project aims

The Pioneers' Club first met in June 2001 and was the result of a Department of Trade and Industry Partners in Innovation contract entitled *Sustainable construction: targets and indicators*. This project was part of a suite of three projects, which also included a sustainable construction award scheme (CIRIA, 2004) and the production of 10 company case studies from the Pioneer companies combined with a two-day industry conference on sustainable construction. As contributors to CIRIA's precursor publication on sustainable construction indicators (CIRIA, 2001) each Pioneer company had been engaged in the development of the CIRIA indicators. The approach in developing these was endorsed by several industry groups and key stakeholders including the Construction Industry Board, Sustainable Construction Focus Group, Movement for Innovation Sustainability Working Party, Construction Industry Council and Environment Agency.

By joining the Pioneers' Club they sought to take the next step in engaging with all aspects of indicator implementation through practical trialling processes. This involved the sharing of experience between the participants through meetings and workshops. The project focused on exchanging ideas on the internal company management aspects of sustainability and indicators.

Sustainable construction

Addressing environmental, social or economic aspects, each CIRIA indicator provides a snapshot of progress towards sustainable construction. Overall sustainability performance can be assessed by setting improvement targets and considering progress against a suite of indicators as a whole.

The Pioneers' Club supported its member companies in addressing the CIRIA *social and environmental* indicators only. The economic indicators were not directly addressed in this study, although related issues were clearly integral to company thinking. As the focus was on internal management processes it was appropriate for companies to amend the CIRIA indicators or introduce non-CIRIA indicators to complement the overall collection of indicators they were adopting.

Methodology and aspects of the change process

As practical experience of both sustainability and indicators were generally at an early stage for the industry, the aim was to explore improvement strategies by sharing experience around the various common stages of change implementation associated with indicator use, for example:

- identification of key impacts
- promotion of sustainable construction internally
- selection of indicators
- development of data collection procedures
- collection of performance data
- analysis of data to determine key performance improvement requirements
- development and implementation of performance improvement initiatives
- preparation of sustainability reports.

It was recognised that each company was defined as much by difference as by commonality, and so the research methodology avoided prescription in favour of more flexible and open-ended approaches which could accommodate learning from varied experience and rates of implementation. This report structures its analysis of this process around the following headings:

Part 1   Background
             – considering the sustainability agenda and the emerging role of KPIs

Part 2   Company starting positions and motivations
             – looking at motivations for participation and the drivers for indicator adoption

Part 3   Key lessons from selection and trialling
             – summarising experiences from trialling and drawing out key lessons

Part 4   Introduction to the company case studies
             – presenting the themes of the individual company case studies

Part 5   Conclusions
             – collating the key learning points

At the beginning of certain relevant sections boxes are included which are entitled "Key practical considerations from this section". These contain learning points that have been re-formulated into checklist questions to support their practical application.

1.2   Key performance indicators

Background to industry KPIs

A KPI measures the performance of an activity that is important to the success of a company. The role of a KPI is to enable the recording of progress (or otherwise) towards pre-set achievable targets for such an activity.

In his report entitled *Rethinking construction* (DETR, 1998), Sir John Egan set challenging objectives for the industry and recommended that performance measures be established. Since then a set of standardised "headline" KPIs were developed by industry and the DTI. Constructing Excellence's website, KPI Zone, contains information on a range of industry indicators and provides guidance on their use (Constructing Excellence, 2004). <www.constructingexcellence.org.uk/resourcecentre/kpizone>.

With the continued industry emphasis on metrics, further detailed KPIs have emerged as tools for managing business and project improvement, and for demonstrating the evidence of that improvement both for internal audiences and to key external stakeholders. CIRIA, likewise, along with the industry, developed a suite of strategic and operational sustainable construction indicators (CIRIA, 2001) which would support a range of improvements in a manner complementary to government policy and reporting aims.

Key performance indicators are appropriate for measuring performance against criteria for sustainable construction and can be used to manage internal improvement as well as setting performance standards for suppliers and sub-contractors.

Defined carefully, KPIs are also a potential route to external benchmarking of performance, enabling well-performing companies to be more readily distinguished from competition in the marketplace – and ultimately for industry leaders to be compared by investors against their peers in other sectors.

However, there is a recognition that construction companies and the projects they undertake are so varied that comparison between them, using KPIs, is a less straightforward process than in many other industries. The Pioneers' Club has recognised that a trial of the sustainable construction indicators by companies in real conditions was a vital step to the wider adoption of the approach.

CIRIA indicators and government principles for sustainable development

The Pioneers' Club focused on trialling the CIRIA social and environmental indicators. These integrate with the following government principles for sustainable development (OST, 1999):

- effective protection of the environment
- prudent use of natural resources
- social progress which recognises the needs of everyone.

The indicator chart in Appendix 3 shows how the CIRIA indicators are linked through *themes* and *key issues* to government principles. This chart was developed in conjunction with the CIRIA's award scheme project (C619 CIRIA, 2004), and, by cross-referencing to that project's award criteria, provides a useful sustainability tool for practitioners.

Strategic indicators

Sixteen *strategic* environmental and social indicators were identified by CIRIA (CIRIA, 2001). The strategic indicators do not directly measure performance but are suitable for measuring the systems in place to improve performance. These indicators apply at corporate level, rather than to individual projects. An example of a CIRIA strategic indicator is:

- percentage of projects that include (and implement) a plan for stakeholder dialogue.

Strategic indicators are applicable to both *design* and *contracting* companies.

Operational indicators

Sixty *operational* environmental and social indicators were also identified (CIRIA, 2001). Operational indicators are those suitable for measuring the performance of the company in delivering more sustainable construction projects. These indicators apply to individual projects rather than at corporate level. An example of a CIRIA operational indicator is:

- tonnes of wastes to landfill per £ turnover.

As with the strategic indicators, operational social indicators are also relevant to both design and contracting companies, whereas each operational environmental indicator is intended to be relevant for one or the other but not both.

An example of a CIRIA operational environmental indicator for *design* companies is:

- percentage of projects for which life-time costs have been derived and were a material consideration in the design.

An example of a CIRIA operational environmental indicator for *contracting* companies is:

- CO_2 released (in tonnes) per £ turnover arising from construction activities.

1.3 CIRIA's Pioneers' Club

Aim, composition and process of the Club

The aim of the Club was to engage in the practical trialling of CIRIA's sustainable construction key performance indicators and for the participants to share their immediate experiences with the group of companies, and the associated key lessons learned with the wider construction industry.

The project steering group (PSG) comprised 10 leading construction contracting and consultancy companies, the Department of Trade and Industry, Forum for the Future and the Royal Bank of Scotland. The project was managed by CIRIA.

Through PSG meetings the participating companies defined programmes of activity and shared experiences relating to their implementation. Companies provided an extensive range of information to CIRIA for collation. Much of the learning was determined by the direction the companies found themselves taking in exploring new concepts and was, therefore, necessarily quite "open-ended" in nature – an approach appropriate to the research topic.

Participants also attended a series of workshops which explored, with technical experts and other industry practitioners, particular issues such as data collection and management, indicator interpretation, resource sustainability and communications and training.

The final collation of information was carried out by CIRIA. Involvement in the Club ran from mid 2001 towards the end of 2003. This publication contains a snapshot of the companies during that period. A number of them have developed their sustainability strategies considerably since then.

In addition to the research process, industry awareness-raising activities were undertaken. These included a number of Pioneers' Club seminars, and presentations by club members at conferences, including CIRIA's two-day sustainable construction conference in May 2004.

The experiences of the participants were further explored through the development of individual company case studies, written under a related initiative, that are included in the appendices of this report.

The results of the project arise from an impressive level of cooperation among the participating companies over a two-year period. In particular members demonstrated a strong willingness to explore ideas and share detailed information from their extensive experiences.

2 Company starting positions and motivations

2.1 The companies

At the start of the project the company participants were invited to consider how they would characterise their organisations before joining the Pioneers' Club. This would lead to an understanding of their motivations and existing management procedures, and the anticipated benefits of engaging with sustainability and KPIs through the project. Although company experience varied, the overall level of engagement with the sustainability concept, and the management procedures in place for influencing change, were at early stages. Company responses, however, reflected a degree of commonality in their motivation for implementing change and the anticipated benefits available from it.

Company motivations for joining the Pioneers' Club

The companies identified similar motivations and benefits that could be gained during participation in the Club. Chief among these was the desire to share experience and knowledge. This was reflected throughout the project by the excellent degree of openness of discussion and trust between the participants. The following motivations were also generally prominent:

- translating sustainability issues into key performance indicators
- understanding the prospects for benchmarking against others
- receiving input from specialist advisors
- setting up an improvement programme with targets.

Developing the company marketing strategy was, at this stage, a less prominent company motivation, perhaps a reflection that companies generally felt the need to first explore practical change.

The anticipated opportunities expressed by the majority of companies were:

- positioning for the future
- assisting reporting
- achieving market advantage.

The following anticipated opportunities were acknowledged by about half of the companies:

- more integrated approaches to company management systems
- better compliance with regulations
- helping to save the planet.

A small number of companies anticipated the following opportunities:

- better management of risk
- engagement with staff, customers and other stakeholders
- motivation project staff
- publicity of successes
- short-term or long-term cost savings.

Characterisation of the companies before involvement

The companies were asked how they would characterise themselves before their involvement in the Pioneers' Club. The answers showed quite different experiences:

- the highest degree of commonality related to the existence of company health and safety, quality and environmental management systems

- about half of the companies had had some experience of key performance indicators (mainly non-sustainability) and good teams and champions for dealing with sustainability related issues

- about half thought they had limited or poor data collection or handling systems

- less than half thought they had reasonable understanding of issues and a degree of board level commitment to sustainability

- there was felt to be particularly limited cohesion between management systems or personnel motivated at project level.

Although company experience varied, average company scores using BRE's MaSC tool (BRE, 2002) illustrated the relatively low starting position of the group as a whole.

Table 2.1   *Average company responses using BRE's MaSC tool, based on nine company responses*

	Strategy	Responsibility	Planning	Communication	Implementation	Auditing
5	Published policy with targets, reviews and active commitment	Fully integrated into general management	Outcomes regularly reviewed against annual plan	Comprehensive internal and external communication and training	Procedures and benchmarking promoted and updated	Company-wide audit scheme linked to review of action plan
4	Internal statement with some targets	Clear delegation and accountability	Formal planning throughout the business	Comprehensive internal communication and training	Formal procedures with routine benchmarking	All aspects of business audited with some follow-up
3	Written formal statement without targets	Delegated responsibility but authority unclear	Formal planning in some parts of the business	Piecemeal internal communication and training	Formal procedures without benchmarking	Most aspects of business audited with some follow-up
2	Informal guidelines	Some informal support	Ad-hoc planning in some parts of the business	Ad-hoc awareness raising	Informal ad-hoc procedures	Ad-hoc audits with little follow-up
1	No written policy	No-one responsible	No integration into business planning	No awareness or internal dialogue	Compliance with regulated issues only	No management audits of performance

Anticipated hurdles

From the outset, members had realistic expectations and were therefore aware that making practical progress towards sustainability, particularly in committing to performance measurement, was going to present real challenges. The commonest concerns at the beginning of the project related to the following issues:

- lack of data
- limited internal resources
- perception of the process being too complex.

Other concerns expressed were:

- difficulty in making the case for change to colleagues
- issues associated with sharing too much knowledge with other companies
- problems connected with running diverse project types of different sizes
- fear of lack of measurable benefits
- introducing new initiatives during periods of organisational change.

The member companies represent a cross-section of construction activity. They are large organisations with extensive and diverse operational activities including road, rail, infrastructure and residential development, PFI and facilities management. They work in major sectors such as health, education, defence, housing and energy and many other areas. Collective annual turnover for the Club members was £6800 m and they collectively employed 63 000 people.

Collectively their impacts have major environmental, social and economic implications, both in the UK and overseas. Club activities leading to actual performance improvement, or even just progress in establishing better knowledge and processes for future improvement, therefore provide potentially significant lessons for the whole industry. And because the industry is such an important player in achieving sustainable development, these lessons are potentially nationally important.

2.2   Drivers of sustainable construction

Various factors affected the degree to which companies engaged with the sustainability concept and the approaches they adopted to deliver and communicate improvement processes, including the implementation of sustainability indicators. This section sets out the context of varied drivers in which the companies participated in the Club. Again, reflecting diversity in company typologies and their operational activities, there were both common elements and variety in what they perceived as priority influences.

Most of the companies wanted more than to just conform with the practices of the majority of leading companies. In fact a number of companies had stated goals to be industry leaders on sustainability and others lent towards this as a general aspiration.

Companies viewed the concept of sustainability in different ways. For example, about half approached it as a collection of single issues. Others viewed it as a more holistic business model. Some thought it required the integration of all existing management systems. Others focused on using existing management systems independently. Perhaps the majority thought its achievement required the implementation of radical change.

> **Key practical considerations from this section**
>
> In developing company sustainability strategies and related indicators, how have the following drivers, and anticipated evolution in influences, been assessed:
>
> - desire of key personnel to engage with the sustainability concept at senior level and/or develop high profile strategies?
>
> - the needs for performance targets, reporting and comparing achievements with peers (formally or informally)?
>
> - the opportunities from integrating different management systems?
>
> - the need to comply, and surpass, EMS and government policy/ regulatory requirements?
>
> - opportunities for maximising impacts from existing internal initiatives and best practice?
>
> - the need for innovation and project/ service improvement through practical solutions?

Analysis of company experience indicated that drivers could be broadly categorised under five main headings:

1   Engagement and strategic positioning.
2   EMS origins and the role of other management systems.
3   Internal knowledge and performance improvement requirements.
4   Company and staff values.
5   External pressures.

These drivers were identified from more detailed sets of considerations as summarised in the following table (Table 2.2). This table includes a number of summaries and illustrative examples selected from the array of feedback provided by the companies.

Table 2.2   *Company drivers*

Main driver groups	Detailed drivers	Summaries of company feedback and illustrative examples
Engagement and strategic positioning	Generalised desire to engage with the sustainability concept at senior level	Companies reported growing general recognition of the importance of sustainability at group board and business levels indicating that the concept, even in a relatively undefined state, was beginning to inform mainstream business issues, with interest being shown in the potential for corporate activity. It seemed apparent that environmental issues were the starting point for most Club members, but that integration with social sustainability issues was either currently on the senior level agenda, or was at least being explored as a business issue, and that a greater senior management common understanding was being sought.
	Industry high profile versus internally focused approaches	For two or three of the organisations, board-level champions had emerged who were seen to drive sustainability, sometimes through senior sustainable development committees with key responsibilities for overseeing initiatives. Such organisations tended to take a high profile approach to engagement and were likely to have embraced more fully the social aspects of sustainability. Other organisations adopted a more internally focused approach locating sustainability at director level and under the general auspices of health, safety and environment.
	Targets, comparing with peers, reporting	Participants were generally interested in moving towards the setting of consistent internal sustainability targets for improvement. They were also interested in understanding their comparative performance against other similar companies in their sectors. One company expressed particular interest in being benchmarked against leading non-construction companies. In the absence of the formal reporting of data against common indicators, the companies were particularly interested in informal comparisons through the sharing of qualitative information. In terms of company reporting, many of the companies produced regular annual environmental reports and a number prepared sustainability reports, a few of which had begun to report data from indicators. External benchmarking was considered a potential future goal for many of the companies.
EMS origins and the role of other management systems	Going beyond environmental management and compliance with environmental regulations	The need to address sustainability was coupled with a general sense that reporting beyond environmental matters was likely to be an increasing requirement. However, engagement with sustainability was generally the result of a progression from initial commitment to an environmental policy and adoption of an environmental management system conforming to the requirements of ISO 14001. Engagement beyond mandatory environmental regulatory compliance could perhaps be characterised by an increasing focus on such areas as material resource, energy efficiency, waste minimisation and recycling, with some interest being shown in related cost savings. From this perspective companies were beginning to take a wider interest through their environmental champions in the social and economic aspects of sustainable development, and to consider the organisational change and internal promotional issues required to develop awareness and practical solutions throughout the organisation.
	Integrated systems	At least three companies were in the process of moving towards the development of integrated management systems (IMS), which incorporate quality assurance, health and safety and environmental performance. One company in particular, which had an IMS in place had taken a further step in developing it into a wider framework for sustainability targets.

Table 2.2 *Company drivers* (cont)

Main driver groups	Detailed drivers	Summaries of company feedback and illustrative examples
Internal knowledge and performance improvement requirements	Need for innovation	For some, innovation was a mainstay of their business and sustainability was perceived as a route into moving beyond 'best practice' in this respect.
	Need to improve understanding of stakeholder concerns	The companies understood that different stakeholders placed various demands on the organisation and that these required analysis and prioritisation. One company developed its approach to sustainability and related indicators and targets based on the outcome of an independent assessment of external stakeholder needs. Others had been involved in internal stakeholder consultations to prioritise issues.
	Analysis of existing internal best practice	As complex organisations there was a need to review continually the emerging examples of best practice being adopted internally. Companies felt that much innovative work was already being carried out that could be said to contribute to sustainable development and that it was necessary to apply more systematic methods in analysing the breadth of this work, and in understanding its contribution to supporting future strategies.
	Project and service improvement and practical solutions	There was widespread recognition that sustainability could offer practical solutions for the better management of projects and, as such, there was a need to trial the opportunities. One company had developed this idea by offering sustainability technical services to clients that were looking to incorporate sustainability into their developments.
	Internal initiatives	Most of the companies described a groundswell of involvement in various environmental and social initiatives. These ranged from internal environmental and office energy efficiency initiatives to external networking around environmental and social issues, sometimes at an international level. An underlying theme of such work was the general promotion of awareness of issues.
Company and staff values	Core values	For two or three companies, their corporate core values were seen to be reflective of the underlying factors that constitute long-term sustainability. One company in particular stressed its role in serving not just as goals for the company to aspire to achieve, but also as "behaviours" that teams and individuals are encouraged and expected to adopt. As such they were seen as reflecting the company's formula for sustainability.
	Staff influence	Companies were generally aware of the potential opportunities around attracting recruits who wished to work for a firm that was responding to the sustainability agenda. Staff were seen to be a major stakeholder and their commitment was considered to be a key force in requiring more sustainable practices from the company. There was an indication that individuals or clusters of champions had significant influence in making the business case or in generally leading change initiatives. In some senses sustainability was considered a "grass-roots" issue by some of the companies.

Table 2.2 *Company drivers* (cont)

Main driver groups	Detailed drivers	Summaries of company feedback and illustrative examples
External pressures	Responding to external indices and surveys	Many of the companies had explored their involvement in external indices surveys such as: Dow Jones Sustainability Index, Merrill Lynch Top 50 Sustainability Europe Index, investor surveys on Corporate Social Responsibility (CSR), FTSE for Good (FTSE, 2004). A number of the companies were clearly aware of the opportunity to become more "investor friendly" through more sustainable practices.
	Growing markets for sustainability	It was recognised that sustainability offered market opportunities. Again this was a fairly general notion. A number considered there were major opportunities from winning work by responding to client environmental and, to a lesser extent (but increasingly), sustainability requirements in tender questionnaires.
	Government policy, regulations and enforcement	Many of the companies cited the policy and regulatory framework as a key driver. The following specific drivers were highlighted: • changes to building codes • waste management and packaging • environmental impact assessments (EIAs) • future pressure on issues such as corporate governance • environment, health and safety • planning control • pollution prevention regulations • climate change levy • aggregates levy.
	Media and campaigner scrutiny	A small number of companies were explicit about the impacts of being the target of increasing media scrutiny.
	Changing drivers	A number of companies reported that the combination of internal or external drivers had changed during their participation in the Pioneers' Club, reflecting changing trends in the market place and a situation of internal flux as they positioned themselves to understand and respond to internal priority issues and external pressures.

3 Key lessons from selection and trialling

3.1 Themes

Introduction

Earlier sections looked at the background leading to the individual companies joining the Pioneers' Club and committing to implement some of the indicators contained in CIRIA's publication C563 Sustainable construction – company indicators (CIRIA, 2001) – in some cases alongside indicators developed elsewhere. This section draws out learning points from how the organisations selected, understood and then trialled the indicators as part of the Pioneers' Club activity.

CIRIA liaised with the companies during the various stages of selection and trialling to draw out the key lessons on the implementation of sustainability indicators. This part of the research addresses experiences during indicator selection processes and company responses to types of indicators. It doing this it analyses an extensive range of feedback information obtained during company trialling.

The lessons can be grouped around four themes which consistently emerged during the analysis, namely:

Theme 1:	Benefits and purpose of indicators
Theme 2:	Availability of data
Theme 3:	Interpretation, consistency and boundaries of data
Theme 4:	Implementation issues

For these themes lessons are identified and brief examples characterising the experiences from the Club have been provided. For each theme the information has been distilled into a small number of key considerations. These will be of practical benefit for those wishing to embark on the implementation of sustainable construction indicators.

No organisation has the resources to commit to the collection of data without carefully assessing how the data are to be used and how this benefits the organisation. In considering selection criteria the Club members each took a pragmatic approach to this question. The study, likewise, did not set out to trial the entire set of indicators contained in the CIRIA report (CIRIA, 2001), nor force a consensus on a sub-set of indicators. The range of potential indicators, which span both strategic (corporate) and operational (project) level, meant that a range of applications and benefits needed to be considered before individual indicators were chosen for trialling.

At an early stage within the study each of the participating companies had made a preliminary judgement on those indicators that they considered applicable. Collectively, at this stage, 67 of the 77 CIRIA indicators were selected, representing 87 per cent of the total number. On average 22 indicators were selected by each company and the average number of companies selecting each indicator was three.

Key practical considerations from this section

Do the indicators support:

- organisational aims, targets, core values and stakeholder concerns?

- assessment of continual performance improvement and trends?

- preventative action?

- existing indicators used by the organisation?

- the organisation's requirements for benchmarking?

- issues that are widely applicable throughout the organisation?

- priority issues for the organisation?

The length of time spent selecting prospective indicators varied significantly between the companies. For some, the decision to proceed with a particular suite of indicators was made over a few months at the beginning of the project. For others, lengthier processes of iteration were required involving the cross-checking of indicator applicability against business units, company policies and values and the capability and requirements of existing systems. The companies tended not to take forward the entire set of indicators that they had initially selected, but refined their selections as piloting advanced.

Analysis of company experience indicated that selection of indicators was influenced by a number of evaluation criteria. These were used by participants to determine the perceived benefits and purposes of individual indicators to their particular circumstances and requirements. They can be broadly categorised under three main headings:

1 **Indicators that support organisational commitments.**
2 **Indicators that support significant existing activities within the organisation.**
3 **The potential of the indicator to deliver change.**

These criteria were derived from more detailed sets of considerations as summarised in the following table (Table 3.1). This table includes a number of summaries and illustrative examples selected from the array of feedback provided by the companies.

Table 3.1   *Criteria for adopting and using indicators: benefits and purposes*

Main criteria for adopting and using indicators	Detailed considerations	Summaries of company feedback and illustrative examples
1 Indicators that support organisational commitments	How the indicators supported organisational stakeholder feedback – something key stakeholders have explicitly told the organisation is important to them	Companies sought to identify sustainability indicators, which linked to their organisational aims. One approach to this was to assess stakeholder concerns relating to company activities and then identify related indicators. For example, Laing commissioned an independently facilitated stakeholder consultation in order to inform its sustainable development strategy and the selection of social and environment key performance indicators. An extensive range of issues were consulted upon. Refer to Figure 2 in case study 6, App 2.
	Whether the indicators were consistent with an organisational target – something an organisation had already committed to do	Criteria for selecting indicators to be adopted included consideration of whether an indicator met an existing organisational requirement. For example, for MWH if an indicator was required to meet a target of the MWH EMS it was selected. Refer to Figure 2 in case study 7, App 2.
	The degree to which indicators supported existing core values – something that supported the general values of the organisation	Indicators were favoured which could be seen to support core values. For WSP each core value has a number of KPIs allocated. The relationship between a KPI and a core value is mapped as direct, indirect or none. The performance of the core value is similarly measured by rolling up the results of the KPIs. Refer to Figure 2 in case study 10, App 2.
	How far indicators helped achieve aims or aspirations – something an organisation was hoping to achieve or implement	Skanska, particularly focused on winning PFI contracts, moved gradually away from the prescription of a suite of standard indicators towards the practice of setting up contract-specific indicators at the outset of a tender submission. Although prospects for inter-project/company benchmarking were reduced, the indicators could be more directly aligned with client requirements. Refer to Page 102 in case study 8, App 2.

Table 3.1 *Criteria for adopting and using indicators: benefits and purposes* (cont)

Main criteria for adopting and using indicators	Detailed considerations	Summaries of company feedback and illustrative examples
2 The potential of the indicator to deliver change	The extent to which the indicators could promote opportunities for gradual performance improvement – something where performance improvement can be reported over time	Indicators were generally favoured that were calibrated to support gradual business improvement over time. For example the following indicator was seen to be of limited value once a 100 per cent score was reached (which could be achieved over a relatively short period), as the reporting situation became static and further improvement could not be quantified: *Percentage turnover of company operations with a formal or independently certified EMS to ISO 14001 or equivalent.* Likewise a 0 per cent score might belie positive development work that was in-train. In contrast, *Percentage of timber used in construction from well-managed, sustainable sources* was the type of indicator that enabled reporting of gradual performance improvement over a number of reporting cycles.
	The capacity for the indicators to support preventative action – something that supported the company in avoiding and, not just reporting on, negative events	Certain indicators (eg *reportable fatal and non-fatal accidents per 100 000 hours worked*) although important, report after the event and need, from a business improvement perspective, to be complemented with a preventative indicator.
	The opportunities the indicators provided for complementing other company initiatives – something that helped companies fill gaps in their existing suites of indicators	The indicators adopted were often drawn from a number of sources, with CIRIA sustainability indicators complementing an existing set of KPIs. For example, Carillion's Company Sustainability Operations Group reviewed and updated its company's KPIs, selecting a range of industry indicators including existing company KPIs from CIRIA and the Global Reporting Initiative.
	The possibilities the indicators provided for benchmarking and identifying trends either within or between organisations	Companies were interested in exploring indicators which had the potential to support project or company benchmarking. Balfour Beatty Civil Engineering Limited's selection approach was influenced by its interest in the production of benchmarking data capable of showing trends within projects over time and of comparison between similar projects. Refer to case study 3, App 2.
3 Indicators that support significant existing activities within the organisation	Whether the indicators related to important and widely applicable issues – for example waste management where even small improvements might lead to significant improvements in performance	Indicators tended to be chosen on the basis that they supported widely relevant/current issues for the organisation. For example, TWC assessed the environmental issues facing its business and focused on construction resource indicators as it found that waste was a key issues across three main business areas: ● construction activities and open cast coal mining ● facilities management activities ● design and consultancy activities. Refer to case study 9 in App 2.
	The extent to which the indicators supported priority issues in relation to other company initiatives – for example a commitment to reporting against sustainability industry indices such as FTSE for Good	A data workshop highlighted that data collected often served more than one purpose by feeding into other company sustainability initiatives and reporting requirements such as: ● Business Excellence Model (BEM, 2004) ● company non-financial reporting looking at sustainability issues ● Global Reporting Initiative Guidelines adopted for reporting (GRI, 2004) ● FTSE for Good (FTSE, 2004)annual company reporting processes – additional headings adopted (including for some companies CSR).

3.3 Theme 2: Availability of data

For certain strategic and operational indicators, data were already available because of the requirements of existing management systems. But the collection of data that required the introduction of new collection systems was less favoured – even if an indicator could support a desirable company objective. Limited data availability was, therefore, a potential barrier to the selection of meaningful indicators. Particular challenges lay in the collection of data that required some form of cross-organisational initiative or coordination through the supply chain.

> **Key practical considerations from this section**
>
> How do the following issues affect data availability:
>
> - presence of existing "audit" requirements or data sources such as EMS?
> - ability to dis-aggregate generalised data to the target unit of analysis?
> - problems of obtaining data from supply chains and varied projects?
> - relating accounting periods used within centralised data systems to the reporting requirements?
> - over-reliance on centralised data systems?

Generally, strategic indicators were found to be easier to measure and implement than the operational indicators, given that, to a degree, the relevant collection systems were already in place or could be adapted from information that was already collected. However, even for the strategic indicators, the level of data availability and the presence of systems in place for collecting that data, varied by company and by indicator. Table A1.2 in Appendix 1, contains a summary of responses to a request to rank the strategic indicators by the availability of data and the related systems in place to collect them.

Company internal management systems proved generally to be important determinants of indicator selection. For example, most companies – both contractors and designers – had either implemented, or were in the processes of developing, a formal environmental management system. Because it addressed so many of the issues relevant to the participants, those that did not have the system in place during the early stages of the Club found they could experience delays in the indicator selection process while the companies worked through the implications of the system to their operations and data requirements.

Analysis of company experience indicated that data availability was an important factor in the number and types of indicators selected for trialling. The discussion that arose can be collated into three main topic areas:

1 **Identification of areas where the greatest opportunities existed for obtaining data.**
2 **Issues that affected the availability of data for indicators.**
3 **Opportunities to improve data availability.**

These topic areas were derived from more detailed sets of considerations as summarised in Table 3.2 below. This table includes a number of summaries and illustrative examples selected from the array of feedback provided by the companies.

Table 3.2   *Criteria for adopting and using indicators: availability of data*

Main criteria for adopting and using indicators	Detailed considerations	Summaries of company feedback and illustrative examples
1 Identification of areas where the greatest opportunities existed for obtaining data	Availability was highest where there was a pre-existing "audit" requirement	Data and collection systems were extensively available for the indicators that related to information required as a legal or "audit" requirement, for example: • reportable fatal and non-fatal accidents per 100 000 hours worked • number of formal environmental or nuisance notices served due to construction activities.
	There were significant opportunities for data collection by identifying available data from existing sources – EMS provided a particularly rich source of relevant data	Most companies dealt with the data requirements by first identifying and collecting data from a variety of existing sources. Boxes A1.1 and Table A1.1 in Appendix 1 provide examples how companies can map data requirements against a range of existing company systems.
2 Issues that affected the availability of data for indicators	The general fragmentation of construction activity could undermine availability of data for operational indicators	Consistent data availability for some operational indicators proved challenging, largely because most of the organisations operated through: • various office locations • different divisions and even businesses • numerous projects • varied project types. A degree of manipulation of data was often required to overcome these.
	Data was not always available for the target organisational unit in the form required	The data requirement for the organisational unit being analysed can be met only by existing data where there is a match with the indicator parameters, which is not always the case. For example, the following indicator requires organisational units with EMS to "map"' onto organisational units for which turnover is reported. *Percentage turnover of company operations with a formal or independently certified Environmental Management System to ISO 14001 or equivalent.*
	Data was more readily available for direct influences	Companies had more influence over their direct activities and therefore in-house data were more readily available than data from the supply chain. As companies had very large numbers of suppliers it was necessary to have cut-off points (for example focusing only on first tier suppliers) which were consistently applied. For example, although certain qualitative information was available (eg through QA systems) quantitative data for the following indicator generally could not be readily derived from existing sources: *Percentage of services by value obtained from companies with a certified Environmental Management System to ISO 14001 or*

Table 3.2   *Criteria for adopting and using indicators: availability of data* (cont)

Main criteria for adopting and using indicators	Detailed considerations	Summaries of company feedback and illustrative examples
3 Opportunities to improve data availability	Benefits could be gained from centralised data systems aligning with the data requirements and reporting periods of operating units	As large organisations, there were significant dependencies on central systems and procedures. It was found that, despite information being available in the central management information systems, it was not always readily accessible for specific business units being analysed nor did it always align with their required reporting periods. This, therefore, necessitated a degree of data manipulation.
	Where there was a reliance on centralised data systems it was necessary to avoid risks of significant data unavailability or loss from the break down of that system	Where companies had depended on centralised data systems difficulties with data availability could occur where technical problems arose with those systems – especially where major new software systems were being implemented and delays were encountered. Such circumstances can lead to major delays to the whole process of indicator adoption and data collection.
	Systematic approaches could help match data requirements against available sources	The complexity of implementing the indicators meant that there were benefits in adopting systematic approaches to assessing data requirements and matching them to data sources. MWH's case study provides an example of a systematic indicator selection methodology, showing how linkages to existing data sources were considered. Refer to case study 7, App 2.
	EMS has the benefit of providing key mechanisms for data collection	EMS was seen as an important route to data collection at operational level, and its absence a barrier to short-term data availability. As the following Atkins quote shows, its implementation was seen as a pre-requisite for obtaining the kind of key data required for reporting on sustainability performance: *"Non-financial project/contract level data.... was never really going to be available early on as there was a need to get widespread implementation of EMS in place across some of the large units before there was chance of getting systematic data reporting on operational issues for projects and the Businesses."*

Theme 3: Interpretation, consistency and boundaries of data

Even where data were already gathered at project level and mechanisms existed to transmit and collate it centrally, a number of factors needed to be considered depending on how the data were to be used. The variety of projects undertaken both in terms of nature and size meant that simple comparisons between individual projects or project trends would not necessarily present an accurate picture.

Many of the indicators in the CIRIA Report (CIRIA, 2001) had been normalised in terms of turnover, hours worked, indices etc.

However, a number of factors could influence project-related indicator data at an organisational level, for example:

- geographical factors – remoteness, congestion, proximity to resources and labour etc
- client factors – the degree to which designers or framework contractors could control certain aspects of the job that were being measured by the indicator
- a migration in the nature and scale of work being undertaken by the organisation
- fundamental differences in the nature of work undertaken across different divisions or businesses within the organisation
- comparison between organisations were also be affected by such factors.

Key practical considerations from this section
In planning for the adoption of indicators have the following questions been considered:
• how representative is the sample site to which the indicators will apply and has a project cut-off size been set to avoid overburdening smaller projects?
• is there clarity on the definition/ interpretation of the indicators' parameters and has the level of project detail to be measured by the indicator been established?
• is the normalisation measure appropriate to the circumstances the indicator will be applied to?
• are the indicators that are to be used for benchmarking clearly defined and appropriately standardised, and are they detailed enough to account for different project types?
• have issues of consistency of definitions and regularity of reporting between operating businesses been addressed?
• are the indicators sensitive to the differences between the direct and indirect impacts of the organisation's activities?
• have "boundary" issues been addressed so that the extent of company responsibilities and control over supply chain activities can be understood?

Analysis of company experience drew out lessons that can be grouped into the following 3 topics areas:

1 **Interpretation and scope in the implementation of the indicators.**
2 **Consistency of applicability across different activities.**
3 **Boundaries of influence of the company in using the indicator to drive performance improvement.**

These topic areas were derived from more detailed sets of considerations as summarised in Table 3.3 below. This table includes a number of summaries and illustrative examples selected from the array of feedback provided by the companies.

Table 3.3   *Criteria for adopting and using indicators: interpretation, consistency and boundaries of data*

Main criteria for adopting and using indicators	Detailed considerations	Summaries of company feedback and illustrative examples
1 Interpretation and scope in the implementation of the indicators	A project cut-off size was considered necessary when applying the indicators	There was a general challenge for the companies of collecting data from hundreds of different sites over a large geographical area that did not previously report centrally. For both contractors and designers a project cut-off size was seen as necessary. Both sought to avoid overburdening smaller projects with administration by introducing a financial lower cut-off point (for example £100 000), below which performance data would not normally be required.
	The definition/ interpretation of the indicator's parameters needed to be firmly established and understood	The parameters of an indicator needed to be clearly defined. Poor definition was a barrier to its use for both benchmarking and non-benchmarking purposes. Definitional problems arose for example with the indicator: *Percentage of projects that include (and implement) a plan for stakeholder dialogue,* where clarity of definition was required for the terms "stakeholder dialogue" and "implementation of plan". For this reason the wording of indicators was often refined by companies.
	The level of detail adopted for the indicator needed to be considered	For some indicators it was not clear what level of detail was required and this needed to be addressed. For example, for the indicator *Average distance travelled per tonne of materials from suppliers to site (km),* the following questions arose: ● Should each material type be measured separately? ● Should all modes of transport be included? ● Should this address where the supplier is based or where the supplier collects the material from? (in some cases this may be the same). ● Should sub-contractor materials be included? ● Should Forest Stewardship Council timber be included, which needs to be sourced from distant areas? (FSC, 2004).

Table 3.3 *Criteria for adopting and using indicators: interpretation, consistency and boundaries of data* (cont)

Main criteria for adopting and using indicators	Detailed considerations	Summaries of company feedback and illustrative examples
2 Consistency of applicability across different activities	There needed to be consideration of how representative a sample site would be	Issues arose over whether sample sites were generally representative. For example the indicator *Number of formal environmental or nuisance notices served due to construction activities* may be limited for comparison purposes because "notices" are relevant to only a particularly type and stage of construction activity or location. The reporting of no notices by a company may mean either good performance or simply that activities or location would not have led to notices.
	The normalisation measure needed to be appropriate to the indicator	There were some instances where the normalisation measure for an indicator were addressed. For example, in the indicator *Tonnes of wastes arising to landfill per £ turnover*, normalisation of waste data by turnover may have limited value for monitoring and control purposes because recorded costs can be out of phase with waste generating activities. A better way to normalise this indicator may be to use "100 000 hours worked" – which has the added advantage that sub-contract hours can be included. In addition this has the advantage that project hours worked are already recorded for safety reporting. More supporting information is provided on this point and related issues of formal benchmarking in Box A1.1, App 1.
	Using indicators for benchmarking would require further standardisation of measures and methods for applying them to different project types	Participants felt that moving towards external benchmarking would require increased standardisation of the measures in ways which could account for the differences between projects. For example, it is likely that benchmark data for waste indicators will need to reflect the type of development (eg roads versus commercial construction versus house building). Even within categories of development benchmark data may need to vary (for example greenfield versus urban regeneration). It may therefore be necessary for each indicator to be supported by a series of meta data that allow for more complex analysis. Also refer to Box A1.2, App 1.
	Issues of consistency of definitions and regularity of reporting between operating business needed to be addressed	Operational businesses can provide good data but different data collection systems may be in place for the different units. Therefore there may be issues of consistency of definition and regularity of collection. These will need to be resolved when the data is collated centrally to avoid skewing the final results.
3 Boundaries of influence of the company in using the indicator to drive performance improvement	The difference between the direct and indirect impacts of the organisation's activities needed to be understood and accounted for in the application of indicators	In identifying which data to collect companies found they needed to give particular consideration to the different requirements for direct and indirect impacts. This issue is particularly relevant to the design context. Box A1.4 App 1, contains a note derived from a workshop briefing paper and design company discussions addressing the degree of influence over sustainability available to the designer.
	"Boundary" issues needed to be addressed for companies to understand the extent of their supply chain responsibilities with regard to influencing and measuring sustainability performance	A key issue arising throughout the project was the degree to which the participating companies had a responsibility over sustainability beyond the impacts of their direct employees. Such "boundary" issues were present in a number of the indicators, for example, *Percentage of staff working with flexible hours*. In defining the terms of such indicators there was the implicit dilemma of adopting a manageable yet limited definition (direct employees only) versus broadening the scope (include sub-contractors) and risk moving beyond the company's ability to gather accurate data. Box A1.4, App 1, contains a note derived from a workshop briefing paper and design company discussions, which partly addresses this question.

3.5 Theme 4: Implementation issues

Once the benefits and purpose of the indicators were considered and their availability, interpretation, consistency and boundaries assessed, companies needed to address how best to carry through their implementation. They dealt with the process in a number of ways to ensure they maintained both control and flexibility in their approaches. This was underpinned by an exploratory attitude and the use of internal iteration and trialling. Practical management issues were dealt with in parallel with cultural issues such as the need to ensure data accuracy and staff commitment at all levels.

Again, reflecting the scale of the task, companies generally chose an incremental approach to the implementation process, allowing time for experimentation, trialling, review and internal discussions to ensure approaches could be integrated with other company objectives.

As well as dealing with the continual need to maintain widespread internal support at all levels for the sustainability agenda, the company champions had to consider a range of other practical considerations. These ranged from logistical questions associated with extensive data manipulation to data quality and recording requirements. These, in turn, required an understanding of the most appropriate collection methods such as manual systems, spreadsheets, bespoke software etc.

> **Key practical considerations from this section**
>
> In developing approaches to implementing the indicators have the following questions been considered:
>
> - are there any requirements for trialling and periodic review?
>
> - are there benefits in restricting the complexity of the indicator and limiting its initial applicability to parts of the business?
>
> - to what extent can existing systems and expertise be used?
>
> - what are the software requirements?
>
> - have data collection and analysis logistics, and quality control measures, been considered?
>
> - is there buy-in from data collectors and management at senior level?

Analysis of company experience indicated that implementation approaches could be grouped into the following three main management consideration:

1 **Manageability.**
2 **Process and quality.**
3 **Cultural issues.**

These topic areas were derived from more detailed sets of considerations as summarised in Table 3.4 below. This table includes a number of summaries and illustrative examples selected from the array of feedback provided by the companies.

Cultural issues are also considered in the next section, Communication.

Table 3.4   *Indicator implementation approaches*

Main issues	Detailed considerations	Summaries of company feedback and illustrative examples
1 Manageability	Periodic reviews of data systems and their benefits can be important in assessing the need for future modification	It was considered important by some companies to review at stages the difficulty of obtaining data, and the value considered to be derived from them. MWH, for example, planned to undertake such a review on completion of the first Sustainable Development Report. This information would be used to determine whether systems or indicators were modified to capture meaningful information on a routine basis in future.
	It may be useful to restrict trialling to parts of the business	To make the process more manageable most Pioneers' Club members chose to restrict their trial of operational indicators to specific parts of the organisation.
	The level of complexity in implementation needed to be appropriate to the requirements	Simple approaches to implementing the indicators tended to be favoured. For example, Buro Happold derived checklist questions from select CIRIA indicators. These were applied to design projects over a given cut-off size. The project leader is prompted to complete this, or explain why they have opted out, at each of the key design stages. Although relatively simple, the information generated was of an appropriate level to meet current requirements and could be displayed graphically to readily illustrate trends. Refer to Table 1 in case study 4, App 2.
	The implementation process needs to draw on existing sources of information and related staff expertise	Generally implementation was linked with other systems and related personnel with relevant experience. Many indicators require detailed interrogation and interpretation of information provided by a chain of data holders from project level up to business unit or group level. Box A1.1 and Table A1.1, in App 1, provide examples how companies can map data requirements against a range of existing company systems.
	Software requirements required consideration	There was a need to consider carefully the software to be used in support of the data system. Box A1.5 in Appendix 1 contains a note on software considerations derived from a workshop briefing paper.
2 Process and quality	The logistics of data collection and analysis needed to be addressed	Once there is agreement on exactly what data is needed decisions are required on: • how it is to be collected • when it is required • who has the responsibility for collection • which audience it is required for • in what format A straightforward means should be provided for submission of raw data (at the point of generation of the data for example), and it should be possible to convert the data into "building blocks" which are amenable to analysis.
	Quality control needed to be built into key collection stages	The design of the data collection and management system should consider the key stages of the data process and seek to build quality in from the beginning, by clarifying "data ownership" and responsibilities and possibly by providing input forms or agreed formats and by providing guidance and support to relevant employees. Data collection processes should build on the experience and competence of individuals undertaking current data collection activities and should take account of where required data or substitutes are already collected in a quality controlled system.

Table 3.4   *Indicator implementation approaches* (cont)

Main issues	Detailed considerations	Summaries of company feedback and illustrative examples
3 Cultural issues	Consultation with, and provision of support to, data collectors was necessary, possibly including trialling to obtain feedback and buy-in from those directly involved in collection	To be successful, indicators need to be valued by those using them. In particular, those responsible for submitting information need to see the value of the indicator and need to receive appropriate support. Such cultural issues should be addressed in parallel to the technical issues. For example there should be consultation to understand any problems with existing systems and the way a new system would be used in practice. Data collection systems often need to be trialled in order to obtain feedback before full implementation, in some cases this served to allay concerns about the extent of commitment implied by the indicators. Box A1.3, App 1, contains a note on this issue.
	Senior management commitment to reporting needed to be considered at the outset	The motivation and senior management appetite for public reporting needs to be considered whilst data collection systems were being set up.

3.6 Communication

In cases where it is considered feasible to collect and transmit data and interpret it in a meaningful way, a commitment to implement a particular set of indicators requires some degree of investment in communication, including training and reporting. There was much evidence of communication occurring in a general sense around aspects that were related to sustainability. The role of sustainability champions had an important role in raising the internal profile of these issues. Companies had yet to comprehensively develop communication, training and reporting routes that exploited the role of sustainable construction indicators. Consequently, Club discussions were held to understand what the future requirements might be.

> **Key practical considerations from this section**
>
> In considering communication issues, have the following questions been addressed:
>
> - can existing knowledge sharing, awareness raising and feedback approaches be adapted to support sustainability strategies and related indicators implementation?
>
> - can targeted training be developed to convey the importance of sustainability, recognise staff roles, exploit EMS and integrate the concept into decision-making?
>
> - has a SWOT analysis been undertaken of corporate sustainability reporting to evaluate communications opportunities from the process, the overall business impacts, its costs, the affects on corporate reputation and the potential benefits of managing performance?

There was some existing evidence of growing integration of sustainability into training courses and corporate staff inductions. This was largely about communicating sustainability principles and strategies and motivating relevant employees to support cultural change. Companies recognised that they were generally at an early stage in the development of their training strategies. During the project the design of future training, and its role within overall communications strategies, was considered in some detail. The discussions are summarised below.

A small number of companies had prepared, or were in the process of preparing, reports on their sustainability achievements, and the trend towards sustainability reporting appeared to be growing. Reports could take the form of discrete publications or short sections in the company annual report. The benefits of corporate sustainability reporting were also considered in further detail by the companies and, likewise, discussions are summarised below.

Analysis of company experience addressed communication approaches in relation to the following 3 topic areas:

1 **Knowledge sharing, awareness raising and feedback approaches.**
2 **Training.**
3 **Corporate reporting.**

These topic areas were derived from more detailed sets of considerations as summarised in Table 3.5 below. This table includes a number of summaries and illustrative examples selected from the array of feedback provided by the companies. Firstly a range of approaches that were already being deployed by the companies are identified. Then the Club's views on both future training and corporate reporting needs are summarised.

Table 3.5   *Communication approaches*

Main issues	Detailed considerations	Summaries of company feedback and illustrative examples
Knowledge sharing, awareness raising and feedback approaches	Project and issues-based knowledge sharing was already well established	There were many examples of knowledge sharing amongst project teams and on specific topics, for example: • poster campaigns on specific topics such as resource efficiency • waste management toolbox talks providing a structured framework for users to readily identify in-house procedures and guidance and relevant published information • extensive communication within project teams from tender stage through to construction.
	There was evidence that companies had begun to use their knowledge management infrastructure to promote certain aspects of sustainability	There were examples where aspects of sustainability were being promoted through knowledge management systems including intranets and other electronic media. Company examples include: • a global sustainable development knowledge community involving three different world regions • searchable discussion fora with comment and debate on technical issues, increasingly related to sustainability across a range of different disciplines • sharing, via the knowledge management system, internal and external best practice information such as community liaison and the use of reclaimed timber • intranets were being used to provide feedback to all employees in the company from high level committees down, including information on sustainability strategy and policy, case studies, project related best practice and client focused subject matter and information to reinforce company core values.
	Management systems were a key part of the communication process	A high degree of knowledge sharing on EMS issues occurred around EMS accreditation. Processes included lunchtime presentations on policies and procedures. Integrated management systems were seen by some as a route to improving communication through the gathering and sharing of key performance data.
	General awareness raising of sustainability was much in evidence and took many forms	There were many examples of techniques for engaging staff on aspects of sustainability: • **sustainability competition** – staff were invited to submit examples of sustainability initiatives to raise awareness of the contribution that the company's internal activities and external projects can make to sustainable development • **project suggestions box** – for young engineers, focused on project specific targets that require involvement from all site personnel • **employee surveys** – to take on board employee feedback on a range of issues including sustainability • **participation in industry fora and R&D activities** – for example, relating to construction materials and general sustainability principles • **company sustainability networks** – one company in particular held regular network meetings which included internal and external presentations • **"sustainability challenge" event** – running in parallel with the World Summit on Sustainable Development, involving presentations by specialists and debates • **other events** – included group briefings on sustainable development and presentations and workshops at company conferences by those motivated to become involved.

Table 3.5 *Communication approaches* (cont)

Main issues	Detailed considerations	Summaries of company feedback and illustrative examples
Training	Key aspects of training	The companies agreed effective sustainability training strategies should address the following elements: • ensure that the concept and importance of sustainable development is understood • identify the relevance of sustainable development to "my role" and identify what individuals can do to help achieve sustainable development • maximise the use of existing systems and processes to deliver sustainability (EMS) • provide knowledge of how to integrate sustainability into the decision making process • provide details of relevant guidance and how training can help "make it happen".
	Target audience	Companies identified that sustainability training is required at all levels within an organisation. It was agreed that to ensure that the information communicated is effectively used to help deliver a sustainable project, training should initially be focused on the "implementor". The role and title of the "implementor" will vary between organisations but it was agreed that it could be described as the person responsible for project delivery, ie the person on a construction site who can make overall decisions. For example, the project manager or project director.
	Barriers	The group also identified the following barriers to implementing training: • lack of client awareness of the benefit of sustainable development • low level of awareness of sustainable development • terminology is off putting • sustainable development is perceived as a cost • procurement process often hinders the adoption of sustainable development – for example, quantity surveyors often are not aware of the whole-life costs of buildings and concentrate on the cost to the project • benefits seen from sustainable development are often perceived to be intangible, it is often thought of as a "leap of faith" as adequate financial risks/benefits are not known.
	Content of the training	The group identified that training should provide: • a clear understanding of the global, national, company and project issues • links to existing sources of information and resources • the business case for sustainable development • appropriate case studies detailing the good points and bad points • tools.

	Format of the training	The group agreed that training must be:
		• flexible to encompass different
		  – stages of construction
		  – organisational needs
		  – delivery to small or large groups
		  – allow organisations to learn from each other.
		• adaptable to ensure both electronic and non-electronic delivery
		• include "train the trainer" notes
		• enthuse attendees to do something different.

4 Introduction to the company case studies

4.1 Introduction

Under a separate initiative CIRIA worked with the Pioneers' Club to develop case studies to support the process of disseminating the lessons derived from the project. For these, each of the 10 companies explored a theme that had arisen in discussions. Collectively the case studies cover a range of project and corporate level issues, with a number individually addressing general communication & engagement approaches across both corporate and project activity.

Links between the key lessons from the case studies to the various stages of the implementation process, listed in the introduction to this report, are indicated in Table 4.1 below.

Table 4.1   *How the case studies relate to implementation stages*

Stage of implementation	Business level within the organisation, the case study focuses on	
	Corporate	Project
Identification of key impacts	John Laing plc	
Promotion of sustainable construction internally	Arup	
	WSP	
Selection of indicators	Skanska	
	MWH	
Development of data collection procedures	Atkins plc	
Collection of performance data		Taylor Woodrow Construction
Analysis of data to determine key performance improvement requirements		Buro Happold Ltd (UK)
Development and implementation of performance improvement initiatives		Balfour Beatty Civil Engineering Ltd
Preparation of sustainability reports	Carillion plc	

4.2 Case study summaries

The 10 case studies are further described in the summaries below and are included in full in Appendix 2 of this report.

Table 2   *Detailed summaries of the case studies*

Case study 1	
Company	**Taylor Woodrow Construction**
Title	Construction waste measurement and environmental management systems – how detailed data changed behaviour
Summary	Implementing sustainable construction practices sometimes involves seeking the quick gains first. TWC found that early progress could be made by linking indicators work to EMS development
Other themes addressed	Waste auditing
Other implementation stages addressed	Analysis of data to determine key performance improvement requirements

Case study 2	
Company	**Balfour Beatty Civil Engineering Limited**
Title	Project indicators for management and improvement
Summary	The trialling of CIRIA indicators on a road construction project provided insights into how indicators could be used to achieve improvement throughout the course of a project and how measurement of the benefits took place through benchmarking
Other themes addressed	Site measurement and improvement
Other implementation stages addressed	Collection of performance data

Case study 3	
Company	**Buro Happold Ltd (UK)**
Title	Indicators and the design process
Summary	Initiatives incorporated sustainability into the design of projects. The aim was to achieve value in designs and completion of commissions to cost/ programme, whilst developing useful environmental sustainability indicators.
Other themes addressed	Applying indicators to project design
Other implementation stages addressed	Selection of indicators

Case study 4

Company	**Atkins plc**
Title	Experience with data collection, management and reporting across different parts of a large multi-disciplinary group
Summary	Experience from Atkins highlighted lessons about the complexities faced by a large multi-disciplinary organisation endeavouring to engage systematically with sustainability and sustainable construction indicators
Other themes addressed	Systematic data collection for large organisations General communications and engagement
Other implementation stages addressed	Selection of indicators

Case study 5

Company	**Arup**
Title	Addressing the sustainability challenge
Summary	The participation of three Arup business units in CIRIA's Pioneers' Club provided the opportunity to identify indicators with the aim of increasing the sustainability profile within project management and at corporate level.
Other themes addressed	Engaging sustainability at corporate level General communications and engagement
Other implementation stages addressed	Selection of indicators

Case study 6

Company	**MWH**
Title	Establishing a system for selecting appropriate sustainable construction indicators
Summary	The selection of indicators is an important step to measuring and reporting performance. This case study describes how indicators were selected for piloting, the first MWH Sustainable Development report and the lessons learned from reporting
Other themes addressed	Methods of selecting indicators General communications and engagement
Other implementation stages addressed	Preparation of sustainability reports

Case study 7

Company	**Carillion plc**
Title	The role of indicators in building and implementing a comprehensive company sustainability strategy
Summary	Carillion discusses its sustainability strategy and its efforts to develop its ability to offer sustainable solutions that not only incorporate best environmental and social practice but also reduce whole life costs and improve value for money
Other themes addressed	Sustainability strategy
Other implementation stages addressed	Promotion of sustainable construction internally

Case study 8

Company	**Skanska**
Title	Winning work by demonstrating sustainability performance
Summary	Skanska investigated public procurement demands by researching key public sector policy documents. It was then possible to take data on performance from the indicator implementation process and feed it into tenders to address client conditions.
Other themes addressed	Responding to client demand
Other implementation stages addressed	Collection of performance data

Case study 9

Company	**John Laing plc**
Title	The role of sustainable construction indicators in corporate reporting
Summary	CIRIA indicators were used as part of a drive to secure a sustainable future in preparation for a period of significant transformation. The group's social traditions and the case for corporate reporting using indicators are discussed. To identify key impacts, and related indicators, the company undertook an innovative assessment of stakeholder concerns.
Other themes addressed	Corporate reporting
Other implementation stages addressed	Selection of indicators Preparation of sustainability reports

Case study 10

Company	**WSP**
Title	Company core values and KPIs
Summary	Describes the process of indicator development and the challenges faced in the introduction of a performance measurement system building on company core values
Other themes addressed	Role of company core values
Other implementation stages addressed	Selection of indicators

5   Conclusions

The CIRIA sustainable construction indicators are generally suitable, either on their own or in complement to other indicators, for supporting the achievement of organisational targets linked to core values, aims and stakeholder concerns. Although adaptation of the parameters may be required to help refine their effectiveness they support continual performance improvement, the identification of trends and the implementation of preventative action.

The project's club approach encouraged an excellent level of knowledge sharing, including a great deal of informal comparison between companies of their engagement with sustainability. The project has shown there is a willingness in major contracting and design companies to commit resources to assessing the implications of the sustainability agenda, particularly where a clear business case can be identified.

Feedback showed that practical approaches such as the implementation of indicators can usefully support company business strategies by:

- providing evidence to customers of sustainable construction capabilities, especially at tender stage
- improving the perspective of the company to the public, regulators and investors
- enabling comparison and benchmarking against external competition
- providing targets with measurement of achievement that leads to changing staff attitudes towards performance, drives continual improvements and supports and encourages senior management.

The sustainability concept is wide ranging and, although powerful in specific instances, the associated drivers are numerous and varied. Therefore they:

- apply differently to the different organisational typologies which span the variety of UK construction activity
- lead to individualistic interpretations of the business case for sustainability – this militates against the prospects for a standard route map for sustainability engagement.

There is growing interest in parts of the industry and government to develop standard suites of KPIs and encourage their use as tools to support whole sector improvement. It should be noted that:

- in contrast to the use of financial KPIs, uptake of existing sets of indicators to measure performance across the sustainability spectrum (societal, environmental, natural resources and economic) is in its infancy
- there is currently no universal set of detailed sustainability indicators that have been adopted by the industry as a whole and formal benchmarking remains largely aspirational
- the Pioneer companies did not find it appropriate to trial a common suite of indicators but were eclectic in their selection
- the lack of standardised indicators is not a barrier to the uptake of KPIs as useful tools to support business improvement.

The industry needs to continue to learn about the implementation of sustainability targets and indicators. The following topic areas, distilled from project discussions, provide a useful framework for companies to address the main issues. The sharing of experiences between companies is an effective route to company learning, although each company must ultimately determine its own path.

- benefits and purpose of indicator
- availability of data
- interpretation, consistency and boundaries of data
- implementation issues including cultural issues.

Communication on sustainability does occur, and is quite widespread, but is either rather general in nature or focuses on isolated sustainability aspects – and, as yet, it is not particularly focused on performance measurement:

- systematic sustainability training, a pre-requisite to supporting effective strategies, is under exploited – although during workshop discussions an understanding had begun to develop on its key elements
- likewise, corporate reporting, a central mechanism in performance measurement, has yet to take hold across the industry, although there are individual examples of reporting initiatives
- there is no consensus on either the benefits and disadvantages of reporting or on standardised approaches to reporting – although some companies have begun to seek out existing models for reporting.

Companies have many existing sources of data that appear to approximate to the needs of the CIRIA sustainability indicators but they need to be mindful that:

- in practice the collection of data for a suite of indicators is resource intensive
- manipulation techniques are required to dis-aggregate generalised data to target units of analysis and to deal with misaligned accounting periods within centralised systems
- some investment in collection tools is needed
- collecting data from supply chains has particular challenges
- existing company management systems can provide a rich source of appropriate data.

Particular lessons emerged about selecting and implementing the indicators:

- the sample site to which the indicators are applied needs to be representative and a project cut-off size is required to avoid overburdening smaller projects
- clarity is required on the interpretation of the indicators' parameters and the normalisation measure needs to be appropriate to the circumstances to which the indicator is applied
- where indicators are to be used for benchmarking clear definition and standardisation is particularly important
- the indicators should be sensitive to the differences between the direct and indirect impacts of the organisation's activities and the difference between the role of the designer and the contractor
- "boundary" issues need to be addressed to understand the extent of company responsibilities and control over supply chain activities.

A number of additional factors were considered by the companies, such as:

- the contribution that trialling processes and periodic reviews can make to successful implementation of the indicators
- the potential benefits, in the early stages of using indicators, of converting them into

simple "yes/no" checklist questions, or restricting the numbers and complexity of the indicators chosen and limiting their preliminary application to defined parts of the business

- the logistical and quality control issues and the requirements for achieving commitment from data collectors and senior management.

In summary, there are clear prospects for improved sustainability performance, and existing CIRIA and industry KPIs provide useful tools for this. Formal benchmarking between companies has limited immediate prospects but this does not detract from the usefulness of indicators in driving improvement against internal company targets.

Companies have different starting positions and interpret their responses to drivers differently. This results in the business case, which was widely evident, taking different forms for different companies. In terms of the industry context this may give an impression of fragmentation. To address this, companies should be encouraged to meet more to explore and share information where common experiences exist.

Indicator implementation will be effective only if the purpose and benefits of the KPIs is fully understood and they closely align with company objectives. To overcome data availability barriers they also need to align with other company systems which will allow fuller integration of sustainability into company data and reporting systems.

There needs to be better understanding of indicators around consistency and definitional issues. Issues of how KPIs operate in influencing the design process and supply chains needs to be explored further.

Successful implementation will depend on commitment to getting the logistical and quality control issues right which, in turn, will require senior management "buy-in". Communications, an important part of the process, needs to be better understood and more systematically applied, not least to highlight existing successes.

Appendix 1   Selected supporting information

Box A1.1   *A note on linking with other initiatives that have data requirements, derived from a workshop briefing paper*

Plan implementation to link with other systems/sources where data may be available through the following systems/sources:

- EMS which is either accredited to or compatible with ISO 14001
- centralised and unified HR system
- centralised and unified accounts/financial management system/utility bills/payroll
- H&S system – possibly with close links to QMS and EMS
- QMS (generally ISO 9001 or 9001: 2000 upgrade)
- supply chain – eg approved suppliers
- training department
- external indices – eg responding to EIRIS, FTSE for Good, BiTC CR Index
- employee or client surveys or site inspections.

Table A1.1   *An example of how a company (Balfour Beatty Civil Engineering Limited) mapped data requirements against a range of existing company systems.*

Data requirement		Source of information
Turnover of operating company and projects	➤	Financial management systems
BiE Index	➤	Feedback from Business in the Environment Index (BiE Index, 2004)
Considerate Contractors Scheme	➤	Manual input from project start up arrangements
Notices served	➤	Manual input from data provided in monthly project reports
Reportable accidents	➤	Manual input from data provided in monthly project reports
Raw material travelling distances	➤	Manual input from site-based materials engineer
Number of complaints received	➤	Manual input from data provided in monthly project reports
Tonnes of waste arising	➤	Financial management systems and data from waste contractors
Tonnes of hazardous waste arising	➤	Financial management systems and data from waste contractors
Recycled and secondary aggregate used in construction	➤	Analysis of financial management system with materials engineer
Water consumption	➤	Monthly site returns or estimation according to numbers of staff
CO_2 from construction activities	➤	Electricity – manual input from bills Gas oil – financial management systems
CO_2 from non-construction activities	➤	Electricity – manual input from bills Fleet Fuel (diesel/petrol) – financial management systems and manual calculations from tax returns (y/e 2002)

Box A1.2   *A note on normalisation and benchmarking derived from a workshop briefing paper, using waste as an example*

As construction projects vary there should be consideration of what information is required to normalise the data (for example hours worked emerged as useful when measuring quantities of waste produced).

Normalisation of waste data by turnover has limited value for monitoring and control purposes because recorded costs can be out of phase with waste generating activities. A better way to normalise this indicator is to use "100 000 hours worked" – which has the added advantage that sub-contract hours can be included. In addition this has the advantage that project hours worked are already recorded for safety reporting.

If waste cost is used in indicators, care needs to be taken to ensure that costs are properly allocated within financial systems. For example, waste costs picked up by sub-contractors may appear elsewhere in the financial systems and not be capable of disaggregating.

As companies develop their strategies and perhaps begin to move more towards external benchmarking of these sustainability activities, there will be increased standardisation of the measures, particular in respect to normalisation of data. This will place additional burdens on the existing systems (primarily spreadsheet based), processes and individuals. For those organisations that choose to move towards public reporting this will be even more apparent.

It is likely that benchmark data for waste indicators will need to reflect the type of development (eg roads versus, commercial construction versus house building). Even within categories of development benchmark data may need to vary (for example greenfield versus urban regeneration). It may therefore be necessary for each indicator to be supported by a series of meta data that allow for more complex analysis. Meta data are data "about" an indicator, often used to record the circumstances, which led to the indicated value. For example meta data relating to measured waste might be the extent to which the client specified waste minimisation measures.

Waste indicators and benchmarks can be used at all stages of the development process (not just for design and construction work). For example estimating and buying may be able to incorporate packaging targets.

Quote from Balfour Beatty Civil Engineering Limited relating to prospects from benchmarking:

"...... all Group companies have collected safety and environmental data for inclusion in the Group's Safety and Environmental Report. This has allowed us to compare data collection processes and analyse results. Whilst a full interpretation of the results is not yet complete, an initial comment is that collection of similar data suites is applicable for the group – but performance between Operating Companies is not meaningful as all work in different environments".

Box A1.3   *A note on the importance of providing feedback to and gaining support from data providers, derived from a workshop briefing paper*

To be successful, indicators need to be valued by those using them. There was a clear aversion to collecting data, even if it was readily available, unless it could be used to improve business decisions and thereby lead to better performance. In particular, those responsible for submitting information need to see the value of the indicator, this is helped by:

- making sure that adequate data gathering processes are in place which support the needs of those submitting information

- providing timely feedback related where possible to appropriate benchmarks (eg last month performance, target, other sites, and industry benchmark).

Box A1.4   *A note addressing the degree of influence over sustainability available to the designer, derived from a workshop briefing paper, design company discussions and an excerpt from the final section of Arup's case study in Appendix 2*

Workshop and design company discussions

As part of their internal management procedure, a number of the design companies had made significant strides in addressing the impacts of their own office buildings. The impact of their designs on their external construction projects, however, was recognised by all members to be much greater. As summarised in the list below there were quite fundamental issues relating to the limited degree of ultimate influence a designer normally has over the performance of a project and its outputs:

- the priority at the design stage is to meet the client brief, normally at minimum capital cost

- most of the design indicators related to the output of the design (eg percentage of projects including renewable energy)

- while the designer has an important role in influencing how an output is achieved, the output itself is more often specified by the client

- client interest in the building costs is normally dominated by capital expenditure, rather than operating costs

- even where the client will operate the building, costs may be passed on

- the discount rate used in making an investment decision means that operational savings more than a few years into the life of the building make little difference to the Net Present Value (NPV) of the investment

Sustainability measures may be "filtered out" in the later stages of the design and construction process. If a sustainability initiative is not incorporated at the early design stages it is not likely to be added later. But it is not unusual to "lose" sustainability features in the fully-costed detail design stage and, more common still, that they may be sacrificed during so called "value engineering" exercises when the tenders are returned.

Another important issue relates to internal and external supply chain management with respect to influence on services and products received, as well as information available about those services and products. The definition of internal and external boundaries needs to be clearly expressed when the sustainability indicators system is set up. For designers, client instruction is often considered the determining factor. Should a client make a request for a certain issue not to be investigated any further, such as the installation of renewable energy sources as part of a building project, then the design of such a system is normally terminated.

For indirect impacts, where the eventual impact may be under the control of the client, the design organisation does have control of the *process* used. Under these circumstances, information relating to process assurance may give better indication of the sustainability of the organisation's activities.

"Supply-side" Sustainability (excerpt from Arup's case study)

While engineers are well positioned to deliver technical solutions that support sustainability principles and objectives, the presentation of arguments for adoption of particular technologies or design options is not always presented in the most appropriate manner to convince the client that there is an associated net benefit.

Given that sustainability issues are often subordinated to issues of time, cost and quality in decision-making, sustainability is often not afforded due consideration on projects. Arguments of technical feasibility, capital outlay, inadequate payback periods, excessive risk and a lack of quantifiable returns often overshadow sustainability initiatives and their incorporation into the mainstream objectives of a project.

The means of demonstrating the value of incorporating sustainability issues into a project is generally inadequate. Whole-life costing, life-cycle analysis and payback periods are most commonly used to support the adoption of design options or technologies. However, where benefits are less tangible or not as readily quantifiable, new analytical methods are required to support the assessment of alternatives.

Box A1.5   *A note on software considerations derived from a workshop briefing paper*

There is a need to consider carefully the software to be used in support of the data system. Spreadsheets are good for capturing data, undertaking quick trend analysis and for reporting "snapshots" on a one-off basis. Problems with errors, data input and manipulation tend to arise as the reporting cycle is repeated.

Proprietary (eg Environmental Management Information System (EMIS)) databases provide a comprehensive functionality for the whole cycle from collection through analysis and reporting. Implementation costs are significant, although in general much of the cost relates to the design of the overall data system (a step that is often omitted with in-house databases at eventual greater overall cost).

Benchmarking software is a cost-effective alternative to EMIS databases. These do, however, require the data manipulation and analysis to be done elsewhere (ie the benchmarked and reported data is in the same format as the input data).

Enterprise Resource Planning (eg Financial) Systems are useful. In principle many of these have the functionality required although there may be restrictions in the fields available to deal with non-financial quantities. They have the other advantage that most organisations already have such systems. Major disadvantages are cost (both initial and operating) and the lack of priority that can be given to non-financial issues. Also they are often not available to users on location at site.

Data practices, particularly manual systems, must be quality controlled to ensure the reported figures withstand potential scrutiny. This is likely to be a significant investment (both time and cost) so prior work to justify the savings and benefits would be appropriate.

It is thought likely that the organisations with more visible reporting intentions might consider use of a bespoke software tool or a proprietary system to improve this collection and management process.

Table A1.2   *Summary of responses to request to rank the strategic indicators by the availability of data and the related systems in place to collect them*

Level of availability	Social (S) or Environmental (E)	Strategic indicator
Strong availability	S	Reportable fatal and non-fatal accidents per 100 000 hours worked
	S	Percentage of annual staff turnover for permanent staff
	E	Number of formal environmental or nuisance notices served due to construction activities
	E	Percentage score calculated using the Business in the Environment (BiE) index of company environmental engagement
	S	Percentage of staff covered under the terms of an Investors in People or similar scheme
	S	Proportion of turnover generated by projects undertaken under alliances or other forms of partnership working
Medium availability	E	Percentage turnover of company operations with a formal or independently certified Environmental Management System to ISO 14001 or equivalent
	E	Percentage of company sites operating under the Considerate Constructors (or related) Scheme – ref, 2004
	E	Percentage of services by value obtained from companies with a certified Environmental Management System to ISO 14001 or equivalent
	S	Percentage of appropriate projects that include (and implement) a plan to consult with the end-user
Weak availability	E	Percentage of projects for which standards of environmental performance and social engagement have been formally agreed with the client
	S	Percentage of services by value obtained from companies operating an Investors in People or similar scheme
	E	Percentage of projects for which whole-life costs and/or life cycle assessment have been calculated and used in the design of the project or in the method of construction and materials used
	S	Percentage of projects that include (and implement) a plan for stakeholder dialogue
	S	Average client satisfaction using the KPI approach
	E	Percentage of projects for which an environmental assessment has been undertaken and proposed environmental mitigation measures implemented

ARUP

Addressing the sustainability challenge

Company snapshot

Company:	*Ove Arup & Partners Ltd*
Operations:	*Engineering design, planning and project management services in all areas of the built environment*
Sectors:	*National and international industry, commerce and government*
Size:	*7000 employees*
Turnover:	*£12 m (three building engineering groups in London)*
Major clients:	*Property developers, architects, multinational companies, government agencies*

Case study theme

The participation of three London business units in CIRIA's Pioneers' Club initiative provided the opportunity to identify indicators to increase the sustainability profile within project management and at a corporate level.

This case study describes the context and thinking informing Arup's response to sustainability and its incorporation into consulting practices, primarily through the management of a project design process. Considerations for future initiatives are also given.

The Arup legacy

Building on Arup's philosophy of "total design", the Arup group board recognised that the concept of sustainability could increasingly drive the company's contribution to shaping the built environment and associated communities. The rationale for sustainability was the recognition that the concept embraces the dynamics of environmental integrity, social equity, economic viability and conservation of natural resources.

The concept, therefore, affects all aspects of Arup's core business, and contributes to understanding the business drivers.

Recognised external drivers include:

- increasing legislation, EU directives and changes to building codes

- risk management of environmental liabilities

- company reputation

- awareness of waste and climate change.

Recognised internal drivers include:

- moving beyond social and environmental compliance to "best practice" by innovation

- re-invigorating and opening up new opportunities through marketing of sustainability

- increasing profitability through sustainable development differentiation

- attracting employees who want to respond to the sustainability agenda.

Engaging sustainability

Arup's engagement with the sustainability concept has evolved through a series of events and initiatives undertaken in recent years:

- **1999: Heathrow conference** – a gathering of Arup people interested in sustainability to discuss initiatives that were being undertaken, and what it meant for the firm.

- **2001: Cycles and spirals: uplifting sustainability** – a three-day event held in Boston, bringing Arup's *"most progressive thinkers, active doers, and a sprinkling of sceptics, in the field of sustainable design and development"* together.

- **2001: Sustainability Task Force (STF)** – established to lead the development of a business strategy for sustainability, outlined in the report *Exploring the Profitability of Sustainability*. In 2002, the STF reformed as the Sustainability Steering Group (SSG) with the mandate to act as an advocacy group within the firm and to provide high-level support to business and technical initiatives relating to sustainability.

- **2001: CIRIA Pioneers' Club** – Arup joined the club to further assess the role of industry sustainability indicators and their role within the company.

- **2002: Boston +1** – a three-day conference to follow-up on sustainability developments and set strategic direction for sustainability initiatives within the company.

- **2002: The Arup sustainability challenge** – timed to coincide with the World Summit on Sustainable Development (WSSD) in Johannesburg. Offices around the world were involved in poster campaigns, a lecture series, and sustainability awareness events.

In addition, Arup has a number of associated initiatives all focused on raising the profile of sustainability issues and reporting on performance and achievements. These include:

- OvaGreen – a group of volunteers looking at improving Arup's environmental performance

- SusNet – the Arup intranet site coordinating information on sustainability issues and providing a skills network

- SPeAR® – the framework developed by Arup as a means of appraising sustainability performance of projects, processes and products

- Printed publications are regularly produced to communicate achievements. These include the *Arup Bulletin* for internal distribution, and the *Arup Journal* – circulated to a wide external audience. Both publications regularly contain reports on sustainability issues in relation to the operation of Arup or individual groups as well as project information

In addition, a number of online periodicals exist including the weekly *Arup News*, and *Technical News* where staff can post articles, which can also go to topical news feeds on the Arup intranet.

Pioneers' Club initiative

Arup's participation in the Pioneers' Club initiative was identified as an opportunity to develop a set of sustainability indicators that could be formally incorporated into business practices and used as part of the corporate management systems.

Indicator selection

The selection of key performance indicators (KPIs) for sustainability was the first and most important challenge. Indicator selection was based on relevance to Arup's business as well as the availability of metrics that could be measured easily. The metrics of the data and how they could be presented in a consistent and comparable way was critical. The specific technical challenges to the business unit's performance were:

- consistent selection of normalising factors such as "persons per square metre of office space", or per "project value" or per "fee earned"

- influence of project size and stage of design on appropriate choice of measurement frequency

- variable staff resources due to project programme cycles

CIRIA C633

- variable material consumption requiring longer time periods to identify trends

- monitoring regimes that needed existing management system support

- difficulty in quantifying "design innovation"

- quantifying the influence of consulting engineers on building sector projects.

More general challenges of indicator selection included:

- additional information required without duplication of effort

- adequate training and support to facilitate buy-in

- the confidential nature of data that inhibits detailed external reporting

- normalising data to overcome exposure of confidential information

- assessment of reporting intervals that have to be agreed.

Table 1 details the selected sustainability KPIs that were used in a pilot project to understand sustainability metrics and their relationship to project and corporate performance. The selection of initial indicators was conducted in a workshop with representatives from three London-based engineering business units. Indicators were ultimately assigned by the project managers after consultation with other partner or team members; and the number of indicators was restricted to ensure that the assessment would not be too time consuming.

The selection process included consideration of the relevance of indicators to Arup's business as consulting engineers in the building engineering sector. Due regard was also given to the issue of data collected as part of the company's management reporting system to ensure coordination where possible and minimise duplication of effort.

The level of influence on the outcome of a KPI was also felt to be important as often a decision by a client or another design team member may affect or override the consulting engineer's recommendation. The level of influence was to be assigned to a project by the manager depending on the circumstances and context of the project.

The integration of sustainability KPIs with the existing company management systems was also considered. Integration with Arup's quality assurance system (ISO 9001) and ISO 14001 system, where appropriate, is integral to the acceptance of sustainability indicators as corporate metrics. A revision of the indicator selection is to be conducted in the near future to ensure consistency with the implementation of ISO 9001: 2000.

Implementing sustainability KPIs

At project level, the responsibility for monitoring sustainability KPIs was delegated to the project manager. Projects with a total fee of less than £100 000 fell outside of the remit of the sustainability KPI assessment. However the project manager could opt for an assessment, if it was relevant.

At a group level, the intention is that implementation of an annual assessment will be undertaken by the group administrator and reported to the group leader.

Table 1 *Sustainability indicators*

Level	Economic	% Influence	Environmental	% Influence	Societal	% Influence
Project						
	Project profitability		Design innovations		Client reference	
	Delivery programme		Building performance follow-up		Stakeholder involvement plan	
	Delivery budget		Sustainability plan		Supply chain audit	
					Partnering plan: extranet use	
Group						
	Group profitability		Green transport plan		Staff appraisal (%)	
	"value added"		Waste reduction/ recycling		Local community engagement	
	Possible job conversion		Energy use measurement		Repeat client business	
	Incidence of claims		Procurement strategy		Staff turnover	
	Aged debtor trends				Flexible working	

The benefits and lessons learned

Participation in the Pioneers' Club initiative has resulted in an assessment of the extent of awareness, and implementation, of sustainability issues in the participating business units.

Participation encouraged:

- consideration of how groups within Arup relate to each other with respect to sustainability performance

- support for the formulation of a local action plan

- setting of achievable targets

- monitoring with varying focus or purpose to be coordinated

- interaction with and feedback from other members of the construction industry

- identifying problems with sustainability performance measurement and reporting.

The project achievements are aimed at encouraging other business units within Arup to embark on programmes that improve their sustainability performance.

Issues for consideration

While the Pioneers' Club exercise has provided the opportunity to integrate sustainability into the project management process, it has also highlighted issues that require further discussion. These include:

- the extent to which sustainability issues can be driven from the "supply-side". The influence that engineering consultants have in decision-making regarding sustainability and the means of justifying the benefits of sustainability

- the business model that is most closely integrated with driving sustainability at a project level.

The following section aims to outline the issues described above for the purpose of future debate.

"Supply-side" sustainability

While engineers are well positioned to deliver technical solutions that support sustainability principles and objectives, the presentation of arguments for adoption of particular technologies or design options is not always presented in the most appropriate manner to convince the client that there is an associated net benefit.

Given that sustainability issues are often subordinated to issues of time, cost and quality in decision-making, sustainability is often not afforded due consideration on projects. Arguments of technical feasibility, capital outlay, inadequate payback periods, excessive risk and a lack of quantifiable returns, are often used to keep sustainability issues out of the mainstream objectives of a project.

The means of demonstrating the value of incorporating sustainability issues into a project is generally inadequate. Whole-life costing, life-cycle analysis and payback periods are most commonly used to support the adoption of design options or technologies. However where benefits are less tangible, or not as readily quantifiable, new analytical methods are required to support the assessment of alternatives.

Sustainability as a business model

The consideration of sustainability in projects focuses on issues that are relevant at an operational level and that are specific to a project in terms of its context and constraints. Responding to these issues requires an understanding of sustainability principles and their application to a particular technical discipline.

Sustainability issues that are relevant at a strategic (corporate) level are not necessarily relevant at an operational level, and this has implications for the model used to incorporate sustainability into a business, and at a project level.

A model based on a nested structure of multiple projects that incorporate sustainability issues aggregating into a sustainable organisation is misleading. Identifying a suitable model that accounts for the relationship between sustainability at an operational level and at a corporate level is necessary if sustainability is to be embedded into mainstream business practices of consulting engineers.

case study one

case study one

CIRIA

ATKINS

Experience with data collection, management and reporting across different parts of a large multi-disciplinary group

Company snapshot

Company:	*WS Atkins plc*
Operations:	*Technical consultancy & services*
Sectors:	*Industry, commerce and government world-wide*
Size:	*15 000 employees*
Turnover:	*£935 m*
Major clients:	*Highways Agency, Environment Agency, Tesco, Barclays Bank*

Case study theme

Experience from Atkins highlighted particular lessons about the complexities faced by a large multi-disciplinary organisation endeavouring to engage systematically with sustainability and sustainable construction indicators.

A quick review of its skills and structure shows a company of immense diversity and devolved management. Specialisations range from building acoustics to market surveys, and from nuclear engineering to ecology. UK activities are supported by a network of regional offices offering clients local access to its services and it has the flexibility to undertake both short-term assignments and long-term planning, implementation and management projects.

Its stated aim is to be "….the world's first choice supplier of technical services and integrated solutions for the built environment" and its international activity is carried out through over 50 offices in more than 25 countries around the world.

In coming to terms with the sustainable construction indicators implementation process Atkins first had to develop the mechanisms for data collection, management and reporting across different parts of the group. Initially hoping to adopt a broad cross-section of the 77 CIRIA environmental and social indicators, this turned out to be a more challenging process than anticipated which was severely affected

by internal company changes during the two-year trialling period.

Nevertheless the company persevered in a structured manner and ultimately made significant progress in refining an effective list of indicators to be implemented and in understanding how the implementation process required constant cross-referencing to existing management systems and data sources at group, business unit and project levels.

Atkins publicity information of sustainable development

The build up to indicator adoption

- Atkins had carried out a number of key contracts for DTI and CIRIA which have provided extensive exposure to the wider aspects of sustainable construction and emergent sustainability indicators.

- There was a recognition that issues were broadening beyond "environmental performance" to include market opportunity, customer interest and the interest of other stakeholders including staff, investors, and City analysts.

- Issues such as natural resource management, CO_2 emissions and community interaction were becoming particularly significant.

How the indicators support sustainability

- The pressure to respond to these sustainability issues needed to be managed at both group and individual business levels in a manner akin to the company's approach to the development and implementation of a formal environmental management system (EMS).

- The indicators chosen needed to fulfil the needs of those involved in the marketing and winning of work, who were keen to be able to present, through hard data, some of the company's aims of improving understanding and performance to potential customers and stakeholders.

- Key data being collected, such as the company's score in the Business in the Environment (BiE) Index and the percentage of staff ownership of the company's shares, were already felt to be useful indicators responsive to aspects of the company's own sustainability. Such information needed to be accessed and where necessary adapted in a way which would usefully feed into the Pioneers' Club exercise.

- Indicators of sustainability needed, where possible, to be collected via existing quality, health & safety, environmental, human resources, financial/purchasing and other management systems.

- The company should try to improve sustainability performance across its wide range of services including design, consultancy, site supervision, direct labour, facilities management and other integrated services. This would require a deeper understanding of the company's direct and indirect impacts.

Only high level indicators were going to be relevant across a group of such diversity, and the need to select and normalise such indicators that draw from and feedback relevant information to the teams involved is paramount.

The indicators themselves are quantitative measures of performance with which progress can be assessed. The indicators selected should, as far as possible be:

- relevant to, and representative of, the business

- repeatable on a regular basis and linked to the annual reporting cycle

- responsive to change

- simple and easy to interpret for a range of data providers and different stakeholder interests.

A single indicator is intended to provide a snapshot of progress in one of the dimensions of sustainability. Overall, the broader picture of progress is assessed by considering a suite of indicators.

There is a need to balance breadth against that of cost-effectiveness of data collection and ease of interpretation. For Atkins, in its support services role, the contribution of the strategic level indicators covering overall performance has only a minor bearing on some of the detailed issues of sustainable construction, but far more to do with the trends in the construction sector as a whole.

The criteria for selecting economic, social and environmental indicators were largely based on the following factors:

- availability of data through current collection systems and the cost of any new data collection

- the utility of the data collected to the management of the business units

- the utility of the data collected to the external and internal reporting processes.

The indicators, where possible, were chosen to fit with the objectives and targets of the group level EMS. It was recognised that data collection and verification is an expensive process and should always have a clear end-use.

Where possible, to add value, the data should have more than one potential end-use(r). The data for the indicators that are shaded in Table 1, proved to be those most easily assembled as they came from existing business systems or human resources initiatives.

It is clear that the "challenge" lies with data collection of a non-financial nature within projects. However, even where the data have been collected, there are a number of issues that are important relating to their relevance to the business and the repeatability over a number of reporting cycles. Some of these issues are briefly covered below and it is clear that for data to be transparent and consistent, nearly every indicator needs a comprehensive definition. In some cases a summary of the definition is required as a footnote to any presentation of the data.

Indicator accuracy

One key issue is the need for accuracy of the data collected. If quality assurance mechanisms are not in place or being utilised then the data loses credence or fails to be responsive to change. A particular issue here is the assessment of utility (water, electricity or gas) usage across a spectrum of offices under varying lease terms. Some utility demands such as those coming from sole occupancy of a building are well understood and can be clearly attributed to certain staff occupancy and known area. However, in multi-tenancy premises the situation is often much less certain and the data reported may be of doubtful quality. The question is raised as to how representative of the wider office portfolio are those data, and is it right to use these data for scaling up to give the group wide picture?

Indicator inclusion

Nearly all indicators lack clarity of definition which often relate to system boundaries such as Joint Venture's (JVs) and their performance. Financial data are separately covered in relation to the company's share in the JV. Social and environmental performance data is difficult to interpret when the company has less than a 50 per cent share of the JV.

Performance attribution

Some impacts are attributable to Atkins and some are attributable to the customer who has outsourced certain essential functions to a third party. These kinds of reporting initiatives are more straightforward for vertically integrated companies but not the service providers. An example of the issue of what is appropriate for reporting and attribution is an Atkins contract to run and manage a fleet of road gritter vehicles for a county council. Should the carbon dioxide emissions associated with the fuel used by this operation be attributable to Atkins or to the county council and be included in the calculation of carbon dioxide per Atkins' employee?

Indicator normalisation

Some data are always going to have to rely on selected samples such as cost of water rather then volume used. Where data are normalised against staff numbers the appropriate baseline may change frequently. Data normalised against turnover could be fees or total budget including expenses.

The CIRIA indicators being trialled

Table 1 *Environmental and social indicators being implemented, with shaded areas showing the more easily managed indicators*

Strategic (plc level)	
Environmental	**Social**
• % UK company turnover with formal EMS systems • % score calculated using the BiE index of environmental engagement • CO_2 emitted per £1 m turnover	• % staff covered under Investors in People or similar scheme • Staff turnover rate • H&S accident rates • Average client satisfaction using the KPI scale (or other systematic recording) • % of staff owning company shares
Operational (plc, business and project level	
Environmental	**Social**
• Number of environmental notices relating to construction per £100 m UK turnover • % of large construction projects (revenue >£1 m) for which EIA has been prepared and mitigation measures implemented • % of large construction projects (revenue >£1 m) for which M4I index of project/contract sustainability has been calculated • % of large construction related projects (revenue >£1 m) for which an EMP has been implemented	• % staff receiving formal annual appraisals • % staff with a pension to which the company contributes • % staff involved in ongoing surveys of job satisfaction • Number of clients with whom long term strategic alliances have been formed • Number of suppliers with whom long term strategic alliances have been formed • % of large construction related projects (revenue >£1 m) for which a stakeholder dialogue has been initiated • % of large construction related projects (revenue >£1 m) for which a partnering proposal been initiated.

The challenge of implementation across the group

The issue has not been the introduction of indicators themselves, but rather the widening of them to include some non-financial indicators that reflect staff, social, customer satisfaction, environmental and resource use understanding. This had to be done in a way that complemented existing practice and sources of data.

The use of balanced scorecard reporting of key performance indicators has been widespread and some non-financial indicators (such as staff turnover and customer satisfaction) have been reported at business unit level for many years. This is a spider diagram approach to representing a series of business performance indicators in a coherent graphical manner to inter-compare business streams and identify strengths and weaknesses. However the establishment of sustainable development indicators has so far been mainly on group level activity. The challenge has been to achieve an appropriate degree of integration of data management between group, business and project level activity.

Consideration was given to what currently measurable performance data were available in a common format across business units, and whether such data could be collected at business unit or project level and aggregated in some manner. As might be expected, the most commonly available data available at all levels are financial and, apart from that, the main data collections systems relate to human resources (HR) issues and purchasing.

With the diversity of activity in the company some types of data relating to sustainable construction were not extensively applicable across the group. There was also the question of the value of data emanating from smaller projects but clearly the multitude of regular "small tasks" such as happens in facilities management (FM) contracts, needed to be captured in some manner.

The business units are significantly different, and the scale and type of services and contracts with which they are involved militates against use of a common set of indicators other than a minimum. Therefore there is currently no wish to identify or impose any set of common performance indicators on the business units. However, common financial and human resource systems allow those sustainable development indicators that relate to financial and "own-staff" aspects to be more easily dealt with on a common and normalised basis.

Where individual business units have also gone down the path of formalising their EMS and obtaining external certification to ISO14001, then the development and reporting of environmental indicators is occurring. However, they, alongside any H&S key performance indicators, are only part of the balanced scorecard type approach being used to assist business unit board management decisions.

A further challenge was the level of accuracy of some of the data measurements which was recognised as likely to be variable across a diverse and geographically spread organisation. The interpretation of the reporting requirements was always going to be variable unless the data were already collected and reported centrally through current verification systems.

Managing the process

Environmental management activity was supported initially by the development of the group level environmental support team within the company's environmental consultancy business.

More recently, environmental management had been supported by the creation of group Quality, Safety and Environment (QSE), within the Corporate Services Director's organisation, but further management changes have now brought group QSE alongside the rail QSE team in a integrated team.

Atkins adopts a formal systematic approach to environmental and quality management. It is working to implement quality, H&S and EMS that are incorporated as integral parts of the Business Management Systems (BMS). Many parts of the Atkins Group have moved to be certified under the upgraded requirements of BS EN ISO 9001: 2000. It also subscribes to the principles set out in the European Quality Award and measures project and business performance using a number of indicators, including client satisfaction.

Each main contract is subject to formal evaluation and clients are asked to contribute to this process. In the Rail, Environment, Faithful & Gould, Highways and Transportation businesses formal third party certification to the ISO 14001 standard has been achieved along with other business units that were due for certification in the first half of 2003.

Many parts of the group are moving towards achieving the Investors in People (IIP) award with a significant proportion of staff already covered.

Being a plc there are commitments to report publicly with a statutory minimum demand of financial and business risk reporting. However, the company has gone beyond the minimum approach and publishes a review of activity. In 2002 it also produced a web-published version of an environmental report intended to expand on the material briefly covered in the annual report and accounts. The underlying data for that report were also used to provide input into the BiE annual survey of corporate environmental engagement.

The benefits and lessons learned

Organisational change in corporate services and the new finance and HR systems had the capability to provide improvement for the collection of some relevant data. These advantages are now eventually being realised. In some areas the kind of data analysis required to support the chosen indicators has not been attempted. Non-financial project level data

were, in some cases, not available. There is a need to get more widespread implementation of EMS in place across some of the large business units before there is improved systematic data reporting on operational issues for projects and the business units.

The main conclusions that may be drawn about data collection from Atkins' involvement in the CIRIA Pioneers' exercise are:

- setting up systems for data collection does not always require significant organisational change as some data is already available through existing systems and the main issue is the need for accuracy if quality assurance mechanisms are not already in place or being utilised

- operational level data are significantly more difficult to obtain than strategic data because project issues need the framework of the business unit EMS to ensure systematic delivery of data

- project level EMS needs to be auditable and tailored to the role of collecting data and the reporting process

- a policy is required on data communication and tracking data through the supply chain and a means to identify strategic partnership arrangement

- nearly all indicators have some definitional problems which often relate to system boundaries, lower scale cut-off limit and normalisation base

- the accuracy of data collection needs to be only at the level necessary to be effective as more accuracy may waste resources and less accuracy may lose the sensitivity to track change.

Balfour Beatty
Civil Engineering

Project indicators for management and improvement

Company snapshot

Company: *Balfour Beatty Civil Engineering Limited (BBCEL)*

Operations: *Civil Engineering and construction, national and international*

Sectors: *Road and rail infrastructure*

Size: *4800 employees*

Turnover: *£460 m*

Major clients: *Highways Agency, Network Rail, County Councils, Utility Companies*

Case study theme

This case study illustrates how Balfour Beatty Civil Engineering Limited trialled CIRIA sustainable construction indicators on the A120 Stansted to Braintree road construction project. It shows how this provided insights into how indicators could be used to establish opportunities for improvement and how measurement of the benefits took place through benchmarking.

The A120 Stansted to Braintree project consisted of 26 kilometres of road construction running through the following geographical features and associated environmental challenges:

- rural farmland

- one site of special scientific interest

- six main rivers

- more than 30 watercourses

- areas of high ecological value.

Although issues of social sustainability were dealt with during the project, for brevity this case study focuses on the environmental aspects.

Collection of data for the CIRIA project was based upon data already being collected within the existing management systems, with some additional metrics that required additional collection processes to be developed.

Data collected against all of the agreed metrics were used to report directly against the CIRIA indicators, and were also utilised to provide an effective feedback process for the project. This, in turn, allowed performance to be tracked by those responsible for decision making and generated further improvement opportunities.

The build up to indicator adoption

General awareness of environmental issues had been established within the company by the late 1990s. A company environmental steering group was set up to develop policy and strategy, and a process established for managing environmental issues throughout the business.

Monthly reporting to head office, using spreadsheets, was established, with raw data being collected by all projects.

Balfour Beatty Major Projects (now Balfour Beatty Civil Engineering Limited) became one of the first construction companies in the UK to be awarded ISO 14001 status for its environmental management system (EMS) in 1999.

ISO 14001 has since been applied to all of the company's UK projects, and in 2001 was extended to include some of its overseas operations.

Certificate of Registration to ISO14001

How the indicators support sustainability

At a corporate level the external drivers for sustainability included:

- government policy

- client influence

- enforcement agency regulation

- the need to further understand these issues.

Indicators were chosen to reflect the company's significant environmental and social impacts. Balfour Beatty Civil Engineering Limited also wanted to utilise the CIRIA Pioneers' Club project to facilitate the development of a common suite of indicators for the construction industry and, if possible, to benchmark performance against previous year's projects and other construction companies.

The applicability of CIRIA indicators was assessed and a number of these were taken forward to implementation (see Table 1).

Managing the process

The significant size of this project allowed for a full-time site environmental advisor to be appointed. A monthly environmental forum provided the main vehicle for communication with project management and the construction teams. This forum was used to review performance and look ahead to reduce risk and introduce further improvements.

The project management system was developed to be compliant with the requirements of the ISO 14001 EMS standard and the ISO9000: 2000 quality management standard. The standard requirements included review, policy formation, planning, implementation, monitoring, audit reporting and feedback for continual improvement. These actions are compatible with the 'plan, do, check and act' cycle of many management systems as illustrated right.

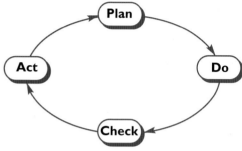

Implementing improvements

Data collected by the A120 project was sent electronically to head office for analysis. This included normalisation by project value/100 000 hours worked, trend analysis and the identification of exceptions. Key to this analysis was the need to understand the relationship between the data provided and construction processes.

Feedback to projects was simple and graphical with the most useful data being used to facilitate decisions on improvement initiatives. The project teams were then challenged to seek improvements by setting targets, implementing initiatives or effecting more rigorous management.

It was quickly appreciated that performance improvement could be realised over a range of timescales:

- immediately

- over the length of the project

- on subsequent projects.

Some examples of the indicators, and improvements achieved on the A120 are illustrated in the next section.

Examples of project improvement mechanisms

1 Design improvements

Reduction in concrete

Re-design of road structures and drainage systems resulted in a net saving of 5175 cubic metres of concrete and the associated release of 1.6 million kg of carbon dioxide.

Sustainable drainage

Balfour Beatty has promoted and adopted the use of a sustainable drainage system using grassed swales to replace the standard design of triangular concrete surface water channels linked to balancing ponds. The implementation of this drainage system has realised the following benefits: reduced demand for concrete; increased attenuation for storm water run-off; and improved pollution control.

Ecological enhancement of watercourses

Elements of the road scheme were deliberately redesigned to enhance ecological opportunities. Culverts were re-routed to become perpendicular to

the road to shorten their length, reducing the length of watercourses subjected to darkness.

Under-road crossings for mammals were provided and appropriate riverbed features were maintained. Where river diversions were necessary the design was agreed with the Environment Agency (EA) and the original riffle and pool flow patterns were taken into account. The use of "soft" engineering techniques, such as supportive baskets and seed impregnated protective matting, was employed for river erosion protection.

2 Site establishment

In Figure 1 below, the graph for waste indicates how site-specific conditions may create increased tanker waste due to a lack of access to sewerage infrastructure and treatment facilities. Collection of similar data from BBCEL's Channel Tunnel Rail Link-Contract 440 project provided the A120 team with good information from which to identify and analyse alternative options. The solution – a small on-site sewage treatment facility, commissioned in May 2002, immediately reduced this waste and the associated road tanker movements.

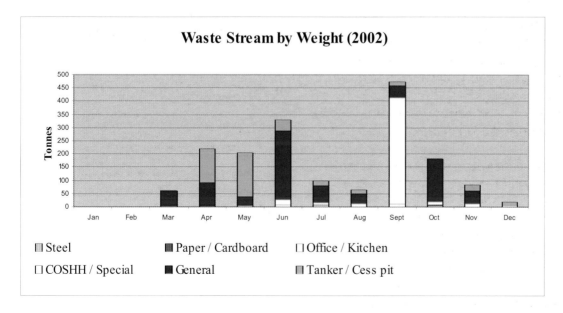

Figure 1 *Project waste*

3 Construction management

Site inspections

At the A120, the CIRIA developed KPIs were complemented by BBCEL's existing measurement processes. This included weekly environmental inspections, completed by site engineers using BBCEL's site environmental standards as the performance benchmark.

BBCEL site environmental standards

The engineers checked for matters such as waste segregation, material re-use and recycling, implementation of silencers on plant and equipment, sheeting of vehicles and water pollution protection. These measurements supported the CIRIA project level sustainability indicators as they ensured that actions identified to gain performance improvement were being implemented.

The results from each inspections were amalgamated on a monthly basis and reported back to the project as a graphical output, as illustrated in Figure 2.

Incident analysis

The cumulative effect of monitoring and measuring environmental performance is the resulting management in environmental incidents.

It is often useful if proactive indicators, such as site inspections are compared against reactive indicators, such as incidents as this can show how incidents vary by type according to construction phase, season and management effort.

On the A120 historical information on environmental incidents by type, has been used in conjunction with live data on incidents (Figure 3), and the results of site inspections to provide feedback to the construction engineers on where effort should be focused.

Complaints analysis

Complaints analysis can also show variations depending on the project activity and seasonal variations and was also used on the A120 to measure overall site performance.

The graph in Figure 4 shows an overall improving trend in performance, and also indicates the potential for increased communication and awareness before the project begins.

Measurement of energy

Project carbon dioxide emissions, as indicated in the graph in Figure 5, indicate the energy usage during construction projects and can provide a pointer to where energy improvement could be best applied. However, energy conservation measures must not compromise productivity, which could in turn lead to an overall lengthening of the construction period.

4 Liaison with stakeholders

The A120 project has worked hard to establish excellent relations with its neighbours and those with regulatory interests in the project.

Community relations

Communication mechanisms with the local community were established at project commencement and included the distribution of 7000 newsletters per edition, local school visits, 1000 letters and a recorded 1500 visitors to public exhibitions.

Working with the regulators

The project also piloted an operating agreement with the Environment Agency to develop positive dialogue between the two organisations and to deliver project specific deliverables such as guidance notes, joint visits and training.

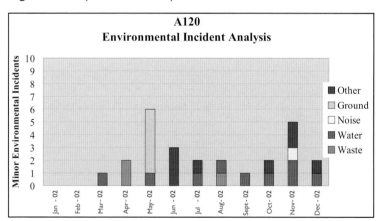

Figure 2 *Weekly environmental inspections*

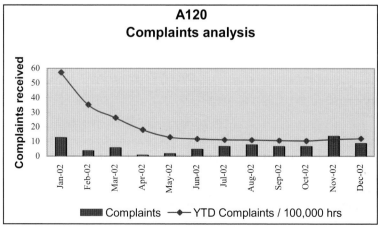

Figure 3 *Project environmental incidents*

Figure 4 *Project complaints*

case study three

Figure 5 *Project carbon dioxide emissions*

The chart is titled "A120 CO_2 emissions 2002", with the y-axis labelled "Kg of CO2" ranging from 0 to 250000, and months Jan through Dec on the x-axis. The legend shows Electricity and BB site fuel.

External reporting

Since commencing with this project, Balfour Beatty plc has produced its first environmental and social report, followed very recently by a second. BBCEL's work with CIRIA has helped to develop the structure of the environmental metrics contained within these reports and provided a valuable insight into the collection of performance data.

The CIRIA indicators being trialled

Following assessment of a range of CIRIA indicators (refer to Table 2) BBCEL is now using the project level indicators shown in Table 1.

Table 1 *BBCEL project level indicators*

Raw materials	• percentage of recycled/virgin aggregates • raw material travelling distances (aggregates only)
Energy and CO_2 emissions	• CO_2 from site related activities • CO_2 from non-site related activities
Waste	• tonnes of waste arising/100 000 hrs worked • types of waste generated
Complaints and incidents	• complaints received/100 000 hrs worked • environmental incidents/100 000 hrs worked

Table 2 shows the CIRIA indicators assessed by BBCEL during their participation in the Pioneers' Club and includes a note on each indicator's applicability to the company.

The benefits and lessons learned

Examples of project specific benefits:

- net savings of 5175 cubic metres of concrete resulting in a saving of nearly 1.6 million kg of carbon dioxide emissions

- improved quality of surface water with improved flood attenuation

- enhanced ecological opportunities

- established a formal process for proactive communications with the Environment Agency.

Participation in the CIRIA Pioneers' Club has provided the following general learning benefits:

- greater understanding of sustainability indicators

- additional learning opportunities

- communication network on practical implementation of indicators and data collection systems

- reinforcement of the importance of a balance between proactive and reactive indicators

- valuable learning prior to publication of external reports

Overall, participation has provided the opportunity to share experiences

Table 2 *Original strategic CIRIA indicators chosen by BBCEL and their applicability to BBCEL*

Indicator	Applicability to BBCEL
● Percentage turnover of company operations with a formal or independently certified Environmental Management System to ISO 14001 or equivalent	Implemented in full
● Percentage score calculated using the Business in the Environment (BiE) index of company environmental engagement	Not used
● Percentage of company sites operating under the Considerate Constructors or related scheme	Not used
● Number of formal environmental or nuisance notices served due to construction activities	Implemented in full
● Percentage of services by value obtained from companies with a certified Environmental Management System to ISO14001 or equivalent	Indicator requires significant improvement
● Reportable fatal and non-fatal accidents per 100,000 hours worked	Implemented in full
● Percentage of projects that include (and implement) a plan for stakeholder dialogue	Not used
● Average distance travelled per tonne of materials from suppliers to site (km)	Limited applicability
● Number of complaints received per project site for noise and dust	Implemented in full
● Tonnes of wastes arising to landfill per £ turnover	Implemented in full
● Tonnes of hazardous wastes arising per £ turnover	Implemented in full
● Percentage of project sites for which appropriate mitigation measures have been implemented to protect sensitive ecosystems	Not used
● Percentage of recycled and secondary aggregate used in construction	Trialled on one project
● Percentage of timber used in construction from well managed, sustainable sources	Indicator requires significant improvement
● Water consumption in (m3) per £ turnover arising from construction site activities	Implemented in full
● CO2 released (in tonnes) per £ turnover (DETR, 1999b) arising from business related non-site activities	Implemented in full
● CO2 released (in tonnes) per £ turnover arising from construction activities (DETR, 1999b)	Implemented in full
● Percentage of staff receiving formal annual appraisals	Not used

case study three

Buro Happold

Indicators and the design process

Company snapshot

Company:	*Buro Happold Ltd (UK)*
Operations:	*Comprehensive general and specialist engineering consultancy for complete developments, buildings and their infrastructure. Sectors: Health, Leisure, Education, Offices, Hotels, Residential, Retail, Transport, Urban Planning*
Size:	*710 employees (UK)*
Turnover:	*£35 m*
Major clients:	*A selection of clients includes: BAA, The British Museum, The Lowry Centre Trust, The Royal Shakespeare Company, Vodafone, Wessex Water, British Broadcasting Corporation*

Case study theme

This case study illustrates the company's aim to achieve value in engineering design and completion of commissions to cost and programme, while developing useful environmental sustainability indicators. It introduces the initiatives put in place at Buro Happold for incorporating sustainability into the design of construction projects. The case study describes the case for driving sustainable development performance and the challenges of designer influence. It concludes with a summary of the current progress and the learning benefits of beginning to measure environmental performance on construction projects.

The build up to indicator adoption

Buro Happold recognises the requirement to understand sustainability and to provide informed solutions through the services the company provides.

The company has an understanding that the industry has to move towards sustainable development. This understanding is based on the shift in attitudes from parts of the industry and the ever growing discussion of the issues in the trade press.

Westborough Primary School – building with cardboard
(Photo by Adam Wilson)

There is a growing market for "sustainable" development to the extent that it is becoming the norm for project teams to discuss such issues even if the concept is not included within a client brief. The drive to sustainability is led from the top with the Company Chair being active in driving the industry forward in his previous roles as chair of the Construction Industry Council (CIC), and chair of Construction Research & Innovation Strategy Panel (CRISP).

How the indicators support sustainability

Clients are increasingly asking for "sustainability" and not always defining or communicating their precise requirements.

Buro Happold is developing its sustainability procedures further within the design process and is researching into good practice case studies. The company has to fully commit to benchmarking and recognise the conditions that allow designing sustainable buildings and infrastructure.

Buro Happold's environmental management system controls the impact of its own offices and the impact of its designs. The design work is more difficult to manage as the company is in a position of influence, but not one of control over the outcome of the projects it works on. The company's primary duty is to deliver what the client has asked for, and if this does not allow for all of the environmental features that have been suggested, it would be wrong for the environmental management system to penalise the design team.

The challenge requires a change to post-occupancy evaluation and feedback for improving performance. This also requires a willingness from clients and occupiers to share the feedback outside of any "circle of blame". Investors, clients, consultants and contractors are traditionally reticent regarding problems where responsibility is not clearly defined. The challenge of benchmarking is to improve the quality of this feedback to the design teams.

Wessex Water HQ – Low energy design and monitored during occupation

(Photo by Mandy Reynolds, Buro Happold)

Buro Happold is a multi-disciplinary firm and as such there are some projects where the basic design performance indicators developed by the CIRIA Pioneers' Club do not apply. In non-standard fire engineering projects, for example, fewer indicators will apply. In some standard projects there are structural and building services activities that may not have measurable environmental and social impacts. In some cases the performance indicators have to be adapted, or their definitions altered, to simplify the measurement.

The indicators chosen to measure environmental impacts were selected based on the criteria of:

- significance to either project or office activities

- company management control and improvement

- availability and ease of measurement

- accuracy

- cost limitations

- benefits.

Because of the focus on environmental issues for ISO 14001 most of the company's measurement has been in the area of environmental performance. Measurement of social performance has been focused on human resource (HR) department aspects.

Buro Happold has developed a "Yes/No" tick box checklist as a first step to avoid onerous numerical data collection on projects. The data are being used to identify trends within the activities being measured in project work. The checklist is tabulated in Table 1.

The checklist is completed at each of the key design stages of the project:

- concept

- detail

- post tender return.

Environmental features may be lost at the detail design stage costing or the "value engineering" stage where social, economic and environmental issues are more likely to be assessed together.

The aim is to set targets for these environmental features once the understanding of the nature of Buro Happold's projects becomes clearer. The results of the checklist information will help the company to understand the nature of the project and the opportunities for including sustainable features.

The process of encouraging good data feedback is managed by the "systems group" that is responsible for supporting the Company ISO 9001 and 14001 management systems. The checklist results are entered via the intranet and the data is collated to form performance graphs as indicated in Figure 1. Up to the end of February 2003 the data from 26 projects had been collected.

The results show that out of the 23 environmental controls, three groups of environmental improvements emerge:

- those that are applied frequently

- those that are applied rarely

- an intermediate group.

The most frequently applied group included:

- procuring timber from well managed sources

- avoidance of ozone depleting substances

- lighting control

- energy control.

These practices indicate areas where projects add environmental value to the construction development and where data is available for performance measurement.

The controls that are rarely applied include:

- environmental impact assessment (EIA)

- reuse of aggregates

- sustainable urban drainage systems (SUDS).

The requirement to undertake an EIA is controlled by legislation, and SUDS is often required on projects, but this depends on the opportunities on the site. Using crushed concrete instead of virgin aggregate can be specified by the structural engineer, but the actual use of the crushed concrete is ultimately up to the contractor (depending on the form of procurement method).

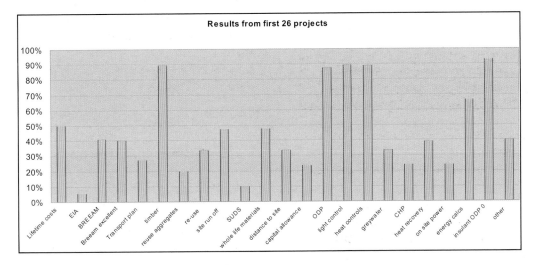

Figure 1 *Graph used to show results from checklists from 26 projects*

Another use of this information will be to enable Buro Happold to follow up on projects that have applied new technologies and provide positive or negative feedback for continual improvement within the design of later projects.

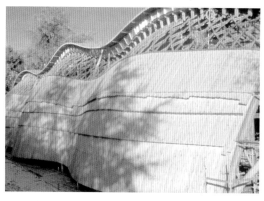

Weald and Downland Museum – timber gridshell building
(Photo by Adam Wilson)

Managing the process

Buro Happold aims to deliver sustainable development as a service that enables its clients to specify and achieve the environmental and social performance their projects require.

In order to manage change Buro Happold invests over one percent of turnover each year into the company's research and development activities. The company seeks to collaborate with a wide range of organisations to gain the maximum benefit from this work.

Buro Happold has achieved Investors in People (IIP) status for all of its activities and is developing an online knowledge system. The company has also gained certification to ISO 9001 for quality and ISO 14001 for environmental management systems within the UK and Ireland.

The company has established several partnerships to help manage sustainable development initiatives that are relevant to the key sustainability issues in design engineering:

- working with CIRIA on aspects such as sustainable construction procurement, designing for deconstruction, social impacts and the re-use of building materials

- use of the Building Research Establishment's Environmental Assessment Methodology (BREEAM) for design and procurement of office accommodation

- involvement in the development of CEEQUAL (the civil engineering version of BREEAM)

- involvement with the design of the Movement for Innovation (M4I) sustainability indicators.

The indicators being used

The following sustainability checklist includes the 23 indicators used by Buro Happold. Some of the questions are based on the CIRIA indicators, but they have been turned into questions, and the requirement for quantitative information has been removed at this stage. The questions that are based on the CIRIA indicators are identified with a tick in the right-hand column.

Table 1 *Buro Happold sustainability checklist for projects*

	Sustainability checklist for projects	Based on ciria checklist
1	Have lifetime costs/issues been calculated/addressed in the construction design considering durability and future maintenance/repair?	✓
2	Has an environmental impact assessment (EIA) been carried out?	
3	Has a BREEAM, CEEQUAL or similar scheme been carried out?	
4	If yes, has a score of "excellent" been achieved/committed to?	
5	Is there a green transport plan for the project?	
6	Is timber procured from well-managed and legal sources?	
7	Have aggregates from recycled sources been specified?	✓
8	Have re-used components been specified?	✓
9	Has the design included features to reduce site run off/water pollution?	
10	Has the design incorporated a Sustainable Urban Drainage System (SUDS)	
11	Have whole-life implications of materials been considered?	✓
12	Has the distance to site of building materials been considered?	✓
13	Has the Enhanced Capital Allowance scheme been utilised?	
14	Have either no refrigerants or refrigerants with zero ODP been used?	
15	Have lighting controls been introduced to reduce energy consumption (beyond the normal)?	✓
16	Have heating controls been introduced to reduce energy consumption (beyond the normal)?	✓
17	Is "grey" water or rainwater collection and storage included?	✓
18	Is combined heat and power included?	✓
19	Is heat recovery included?	✓
20	Is on-site energy generation included? (eg PV, wind, biomass…)	✓
21	Has energy consumption been calculated/predicted?	✓
22	Have insulants with zero ODP been specified?	
23	Any other features?	

The benefits and lessons learned

To understand the opportunities for improving the environmental performance of projects, there is a requirement to get good data from projects and the resources to interpret and use the data most effectively in the management of sustainable development. The environmental checklist is the first step in the process of finding opportunities to add environmental features into projects and it is also a way to raise awareness of environmental issues.

Project leaders and engineers often are not involved in liaison with the planning authorities or the EIA. These strategic sustainability issues often are dealt with by architects, planning consultants or by the environmental consultancy coordinating the EIA.

Specific sustainable technologies, such as SUDS, are often demanded on projects and where they are not, the environmental checklist will help to raise awareness. It has already prompted leaders of projects to ask questions about some of the issues raised in the checklist and has improved their awareness of these issues.

The checklist is a pointer to current practice in applying sustainability tools, where environmental data exists and where there is a requirement for the application of key performance data and improvement.

case study four

case study four

CIRIA

carillion

The role of indicators in building and implementing a comprehensive company sustainability strategy

Company snapshot

Company: Carillion plc
Operations: Project Finance, Facilities
                   Management, Support Services, Road
                   & Rail Infrastructure, Construction.
Sectors: Retail & Commercial Building,
                   Transport, Healthcare and Public
                   Private Partnership projects. (Carillion
                   operates internationally)
Size: 14 000 employees
Turnover: £1974 m
Major clients: NHS (pioneering Private Finance
                   Initiative projects), Network Rail,
                   MoD, Highways Agency

Case study theme

This case study looks at the role of sustainable construction indicators in building a comprehensive company sustainability strategy. Over the past two years Carillion has developed its ability to offer sustainable solutions that not only incorporate best environmental and social practice, but also reduce whole-life costs and improve value for money.

This has been done by using a model, published in its 2001 sustainability report, that linked sustainability targets to business strategy and financial objectives. The process was supported by analysis of the costs and benefits of sustainable solutions.

By using indicators to monitor and measure its progress, the organisation has benefited from greater innovation, enhanced individual and corporate responsibility and improved product delivery in both construction and maintenance activities. The strategy model demonstrates that by integrating sustainability with business strategy through the use of key performance indicators (KPIs), benefits can be gained by businesses and communities.

The build up to indicator adoption

In the early 1990s the construction industry was the target of increasing media scrutiny as a result of protests over a number of controversial road construction projects. To raise the profile of environmental concerns surrounding the projects, environmental pressure groups initiated direct action on sites.

Some protestors also bought shares in construction companies to enable them to attend annual general meetings and pose probing environmental questions to senior board members. This direct approach highlighted that environmental concerns about construction activities were at the forefront of stakeholder perception and therefore, could genuinely affect an organisation's "licence to operate".

This was the catalyst which initiated Carillion's (then operating as Tarmac Construction) journey towards sustainable development and prompted the company to begin to assess and respond to the environmental impacts of its operations.

➲   The development and publication of an environmental policy was an early and significant step.

➲   Appointment of an independent advisory panel providing strategic guidance and support to develop environmental management systems with objectives and targets

➲   Formation of an environmental strategy

➲   In 1995 production by the advisory panel of the company's first environment report, which was also the first published for the construction sector.

➲   Environmental issues introduced to project management plans and meeting agendas and the first environmental advisors were brought into the company.

➲   In 1998 Crown House Engineering Manufacturing Centre became the first business unit to achieve certification to ISO 14001 and the first UK mechanical and electrical engineering business to do so

➲   Decision that all business units within the newly formed Carillion should implement an environmental management system compliant with the ISO 14001 standard by the end of 2002

➲   90% of the company compliant with the ISO 14001 standard by the start of 2003, with the system providing the basic framework for the setting of continual improvement targets.

Figure 1 *Stages of engagement in sustainability*

In moving forward, Carillion's vision was to be:
"... a company renowned for working in a spirit of openness, collaboration and mutual dependency to deliver solutions that ensure our customers' success becomes our success".

How the indicators support sustainability

Carillion's environmental programme has developed and evolved into its sustainability programme and has brought together the vision, values and objectives of its business under the guiding principle of "sustainable solutions for the way we live". Part of this development has been the realisation of the need to, and value to be gained from, comparing its performance against not only competitors in the same industry but also against companies in other industries.

Carillion's performance is now gauged through its annual sustainability targets. During 2002 this has consisted of:

- six corporate sustainability objectives

- supported by 14 sustainability targets

- which in turn were supported by key performance indicators

- these aligned with the business strategy.

Carillion identified its sustainability impacts in line with the government's four themes for sustainability which provided a consistent approach and helped the company better understand the concept of sustainable development. This, however, had to be supported by the business case for sustainable development through the quantification of its costs and benefits. The use of sustainable construction indicators is a key part of this process.

The challenge of implementation across the company

To ensure that the corporate objectives and targets are fully embedded into the culture of the business, the company consults various groups within Carillion before any target can be accepted. The diagram (Figure 2) shows the consultation process that was carried out in finalising its 2003 objectives and targets.

In addition to the corporate objectives and targets each business group sets specific ISO 14001 objectives and targets. These targets are designed to control and minimise the specific environmental issues associated with the activities of the individual business groups and are in line with the focus of the corporate objectives and targets.

Figure 2 *Managing the process*

Carillion's commitment to Environmental and
Sustainability issues is from a combination of both
"top down" and "bottom up" communications. While
forging links with groups such as Business in the
Community (BitC) and the Pioneers' Club has
allowed the company to try to explain, measure and
communicate its impact on society. A key part of this
explanation has been the development of its strategic
KPIs that have helped it learn how its business can
improve its impact.

Benefits of the indicators being used

Carillion has identified six broad categories to
demonstrate the business benefit of taking a
sustainable approach. The categories are listed
(Figure 3), with examples of how they are delivered
on contracts and projects.

Reduced cost	• Self sufficient materials – Vast quantities of material have been sourced from within the site boundary on the M6 Toll Road, as well as the use of secondary aggregate. This reduces the extraction of raw materials, vehicle movements and associated impacts. 5000 m³ of vegetation clearance material mulched and added to topsoil and 2.3 m tonnes of sand and gravel
	• Effective water management – Carillion Services has worked with Colchester General Hospital to reduce water consumption. Carillion undertook surveys of the distribution pipework and was able to reduce the monthly water utilisation and hence reduce the costs from £1500 to £159 a month
Reduced pollution risk	• Environmental Management Systems – Carillion Rail is now using biodegradable products in an effort to reduce the environmental impact of spillages, and has decided to replace the use of traditional oils and greases used in switch lubrication with a biodegradable alternative.
	• Exceeding legislative requirements – Following a review of oils storage facilities Carillion Rail has improved bunding to exceed legislative requirements which has resulted in a reduced pollution risk and eliminating the need to dispose of more than £2000 of contaminated rain water a year.
Improved customer relations	• One of the UK's most sustainable buildings – The Great Western Hospital in Swindon which recently received top marks from the Building Research Establishment as one of the UK's most sustainable buildings. As soon as Carillion became involved in the £100 m project, the company set about working with its supply chain in sustainable construction principles. The result was a focus on selecting different building products and devising new methods of construction. These methods consume less energy and fewer materials, produce less waste and lead to long-term reductions in running costs, which, in the case of this project, already amount to quantifiable savings of £1.8 m.
Improved community relations	• Development of a Stakeholder Map – One of its group sustainability targets for 2002 was to develop a stakeholder map – this opportunity has been used to identify all stakeholders, with the aim of planning dialogue with them during 2003.
	• Reading between the lines – Carillion Building Special Projects helped improve the reading skills of children from Saint Thomas Moore Primary School in Cheltenham through a BITC "paired reading" initiative. The pupils also visited the GCHQ site in Cheltenham for a lesson on site safety.
Effective supply chain management	• Greening its supply chain – A supplier training day was held to communicate the company's sustainability strategy. This encouraged key suppliers to embrace the concept of Sustainable Development.
	• Recycled manhole covers – Capital projects at the Nottingham Express Transit is using recycled plastic manhole chamber segments. Their use eliminates the impact from concrete manufacture, use of virgin aggregates and landfill space, as the previous chambers were made from one tonne of reinforced in-situ concrete.
Improved employee box motivation	• Training – The company has a wide range of training tools available to all staff, including intranet learning modules, tool talks, environmental coordinator workshops and formal training, all targeted at improving the awareness and competencies of the workforce.
	• To recognise employees who live the company's core values, which embrace the principles of sustainable development, the Values Award Scheme was developed. During 2002 271 staff were awarded Value Awards for clear demonstration of individuals and projects demonstrating company values.

Figure 3

The benefits and lessons learned

Carillion does not believe it can yet provide the definitive sustainability solution for all employees, contracts, stakeholders, NGOs, government or alliance partners. However there is a conviction that it is able to provide sustainable solutions in many areas, such as health and safety, staff training, engagement with communities and improvement in site environmental performance through the continued improvement of environmental management systems.

As the understanding of the interactions between social, economic and environmental aspects of sustainable development increase, the company intends to deepen and broaden the scope and impact of its strategy into the future.

Samples of the benefits that have been identified so far are listed below:

- through the implementation of the Green Transport Plan, the carbon dioxide emissions due to company car mileage has been reduced by 20%

- head office energy consumption reduced by 5% and carbon dioxide emissions by 15%

- production of a case study on The Great Western Hospital, which demonstrated quantifiable savings of £1.8 m due to sustainability initiatives. This includes designs that consume 30% less energy and emit 35% less carbon dioxide compared with a typical hospital

- over 1% of profit, in cash or in-kind were donated to community and environmental initiatives

- 2327 formal training days were provided to staff

- zero environmental prosecutions in 2001–2002

Some of the lessons learned are listed below:

- keep communications on sustainability, clear, concise and consistent – this allows knowledge and awareness to build up over time across the whole company

- use flagship projects to highlight progress on your chosen objectives and publicise the results

- vital for senior management to buy into the process and realise the business benefits that the programme brings.

case study five

case study five

The role of sustainability indicators in corporate reporting

Company snapshot

Company: *John Laing plc*
Operations: *Construction, homes, property, investments*
Sectors: *Defence, road & rail, private and social housing, property*
Size: *Over 10 000 employees in 2000*
Turnover: *Over £1500 m in 2000*
Major clients: *NHS, Highways Agency, Defence Estates, Railtrack, BAA, housing authorities, Metropolitan Police*

Case study theme

John Laing plc started to use a selection of CIRIA performance indicators, as part of a drive to secure a sustainable future for as many stakeholders as possible in preparation for a period of significant transformation and new ownership.

This case study summarises the group's social traditions and the case for and role of increased corporate sustainability reporting using indicators in order to:

- demonstrate industry leadership on sustainability

- document progress in implementing sustainability policies through a range of existing management systems

- support the setting of initial internal benchmarks

- to gain external acknowledgement of its achievements against a range of sustainability rating processes (for example BiE's Index of Social & Environmental Engagement and the FTSE for Good index)

A useful by-product of the process was having data available which could be readily fed into tenders for clients requiring evidence of sustainable construction performance.

The case study records the challenges of implementing new policies and the barriers to change management.

The build up to indicator adoption

Laing was among the first organisations to provide holidays with pay, company pensions, bonus payments and shareholding opportunities for employees. The company also had a record of contributions to charities.

A community affairs policy committed the company to working with voluntary organisations to aid disadvantaged people by encouraging:

- education and training

- community regeneration

- better living/working environments

- a community spirit for economic well-being.

Although this policy did not have specific targets, Laing Partnership Housing put this policy into practice through urban regeneration projects, rebuilding some of the most deprived city estates such as Peckham.

The group had supported improved control over the impact of its construction and building projects through the establishment of the Laing Technology Group (LTG) Environmental Services founded in the 1970s.

Further improvement of environmental performance across the group was controlled by an environmental committee from 1990. By 1999 this committee developed a sustainable development policy and became the Sustainable Development Steering Group (SDSG). By the beginning of 2000 Laing Technology Group was the first unit within the group which gained ISO 14001 EMS certification. During this period Laing began working on the original CIRIA indicators project.

The construction sector had experienced a difficult decade in terms of economic performance, employment, business risk and cultural change. Within the group, phases of re-structuring had taken place and there was a continual need to:

- comply with increasing environmental legislation

- measure the business response to carbon tax, landfill tax, aggregates tax and the climate change levy

- track and respond to stakeholder concerns

- implement increasing, design, planning and building regulations

- join voluntary agreements on corporate reporting

- meet the requirements of socially responsible index series, such as the FTSE4 Good, in terms of social policies, management systems and reporting

The company engaged in the following initiatives (Figure 1) to be able to respond to these pressures and improve its knowledge of key sustainability issues:

⮱ Sir Martin Laing chaired the Sustainable Construction Focus Group. It produced, "Towards Sustainability" which promoted the business case and encouraged industry performance measurement.

⮱ Worked with the World Business Council for Sustainable Development to develop closer cooperation between business, government etc, focusing on leadership, policy, best practice and global networks.

⮱ Explored the implications of sustainability through Forum For the Future's Green Futures Business Network.

⮱ Participated with the community affairs division of Business in the Community who actively engaged in partnerships to tackle disadvantaged groups and create enterprising communities.

⮱ Participated in the Major Contractors Group Survey of Corporate Environmental Engagement using the Business in the Environment Index.

⮱ Laing Homes became a member of the WWF 95+ Buyer's Group which was committed to improving forestry practices by increasing wood and wood products purchasing from well-managed forests.

⮱ Laing Property participated in the development of the Building Research Establishment's environmental profiling software tool for indicating the sustainable performance of buildings.

⮱ Undertook a detailed survey to understand independent stakeholder concerns. The results of this survey are summarised in the table below.

Figure 1 *Steps in Laing's engagement with sustainability*

As a result of this activity the groundwork had been completed to the point where it was time to measure and monitor performance.

How the indicators support sustainability

Business development teams became aware of:

- prime contracting process introducing more sophisticated questions on sustainable construction performance, including evidence of social and environmental performance indicators and reporting

- increased number of environmental questions within public sector client tenders (eg NHS, Defence Estates)

- the change in type of questions from "proof of policy", "environmental management systems" and "plans" to proof of "implementation" and case studies

- a greater percentage of tender points being awarded to sustainable development performance.

The company began to recognise the importance to winning business of being able to report on sustainability performance. Adopting a systematic approach, John Laing plc decided to undertake a survey of stakeholder concerns. The purpose of this was to focus on priority areas against which indicators of sustainability performance could be assigned. This would form the framework for performance measurement where targets were set and improvement quantified on a regular and continual basis.

Once captured within a sustainability report information essential to preparing successful bids would then be available in an appropriate and readily available format for "cutting and pasting" during tender preparation.

The process of selecting sustainability indicators began with an assessment of stakeholder concerns.

Laing adopted a novel approach by engaging independent consultants to scope and assess stakeholder views. Stakeholders were encouraged to express views on the broader environmental and social impacts of four areas of operation:

- homes

- construction

- property

- investment.

For the stakeholder consultation process similar activities were paired as shown in the Figure 2 below.

The concerns that arose from this activity are summarised in Figure 2 which also indicates how Laing addressed the need for measurement and indicators for particular concerns.

The reporting process broadly followed by John Laing plc can be summarised as follows:

Relationship of stakeholder concerns to CIRIA indicators	Pair 1 concerns Homes & construction		Pair 2 concerns Property & investments	
	Environmental	Social	Environmental	Social
Could not be measured in the first year	• Flooding	• Customer relations • Mixed use developments • Affordable housing	• The Green Belt • Land procurement within the Green Belt • Ethical investment • Research	• Self build • Mixed use developments • Social housing • Quality & low-cost • Private funding • Toll roads
Measurement was possible with relative ease but were not measured in the first year	• Habitat loss	• Equal opportunities	None expressed	• Local community
Assigned a CIRIA indicator, measured and reported	• Waste • Energy loss • CO_2 emissions • Brownfield sites • Compliance	• Local community • Skills shortages • Training	• Contaminated land • Design • Training • Improvement	None expressed

Figure 2 *Summary of independent stakeholder concerns*

case study six

Stakeholder survey of issues

↓

Select appropriate indicators for issues

↓

Report on sustainability performance improvement

↓

Feed information into tenders

The indicators being trialled

CIRIA indicators that were useful for the reporting process and that the company was able to collect with some ease are shown in Figure 3 below.

This list is not definitive as other CIRIA indicators were drawn upon from time to time. Further development work was required to establish data collection systems for some indicators in particular and, therefore, these were not used in the early stages of reporting.

CIRIA strategic social	Reporting year		
	1	2	3
● Fatal accidents/100 000 working hours	1	0	0
● Non-fatal accidents/100 000 working hours	163	194	130
● % of staff covered Investors in People	0	0	22
● % annual permanent staff turnover	36%	6%	23%
CIRIA strategic environmental	**Reporting year**		
	1	2	3
● % turnover of construction certified EMS to ISO 14001	0	0.73	10.3
● Group convictions/Notices For Environment & nuisance	2	0	0
● % average score on the Business in the Environment index Group	54%	53%	67%
● % of suitable sites – Considerate Constructor Scheme	37%	72%	50%
CIRIA operational environmental	**Reporting year**		
	1	2	3
● % Forestry Stewardship Council timber from well managed forests	Data not centrally reported	Data not centrally reported	9%
● % of projects with mitigation measures implemented (brownfield) (biodiversity)	No data	No data	65%
Other strategic and operational environmental	**Reporting year**		
	1	2	3
● Considerate Constructor Scheme awards Gold	3	2	1
Silver	2	2	1
Bronze	0	0	5
● WWF Star Rating performance	2	2	3
● Skip expenditure/construction material spend	No data	£3.5m/ £55m	£2.3m/ no data

Figure 3 *Initial list of indicators adopted.*

CIRIA C633

For those indicators which could be measured and reported against, data was collected from previous years to establish a base line. These indicators and an interpretation of the data are documented within the "Sustainability" web-based report for 2000 at www.laing.com This data gave John Laing plc an early opportunity to measure performance.

However, some numerical targets could not be set because of the lack of data collection systems or the uncertainty of the company's future strategy and structure.

Other data were available, but required more effort to collect, such as that which had to be collected from offices and the car fleet. Much of these data needed processing and had to be normalised.

Building on BRE and the Global Reporting Initiatives (GRI) the company used benchmarking software to monitor office performance against several indicators and, overall, the company performed well against other similar UK offices:

- carbon emissions were relatively low because of good office insulation, a gas fired heating system and low energy lighting installations

- no office cooling systems contained refrigerants with ozone depleting substances

- sensors for toilets improved water conservation

- waste recycling arrangements were relatively good

- however, public transport was rated low because of the edge of town location

The challenge of reporting across the group

The group was at a relatively early stage of its sustainable development policy implementation. It was not possible to benchmark – either internally or with other companies – in terms of social and environmental performance.

Annual reporting on sustainable construction indicators had not been attempted before.

Sustainable development awareness, across the whole company, at all levels, was limited mainly to directors, group sub-committees and business development activities.

Some of the main barriers to change were:

- change initiative fatigue due to quality and risk management systems being introduced in recent years

- the collection of performance data being considered outside of the core business

- project partners not agreeing to share the costs of integrating management systems or innovative technology to achieve improved performance

- longer-term planning issues

- data collection from hundreds of site-based projects over a large geographical area

The company was able largely to address these barriers by introducing business and culture change initiatives, working through partnerships with BiE, CIRIA and others and using existing management systems for reporting purposes.

Managing the process

Internally, there was a need for all employees to understand their social and environmental responsibilities within the construction process and to the residential and business communities.

The businesses did well in responding to increasing external sustainable design requirements through planning control and building regulations.

The sustainable development policy (1999), set an objective "to work with clients, consultants, suppliers and subcontractors to establish partnerships, designed to develop and progress sustainable construction and environmental best practice".

The business began to recognise the additional cost to the construction process and how this was linked with the longer-term benefits to communities and the environment, within the full life cycle of its developments. However, these costs and benefits, were not being measured or could not be measured by traditional accounting methods.

In recent years, internal initiatives for sustainability within John Laing plc were driven by the chairman at board level and the sustainable development steering group. Initiatives were championed through the Laing Technology Group (LTG) Environmental Department, Community Affairs and sub-committees within the construction, homes, property and investment operations. The sub-committees communicated through human resources, training, health and safety, quality and risk management systems and personnel.

The challenge was to initiate an "integrated sustainability management system" so that changes required from external pressures would be achieved more quickly and economically. It was to improve communication, share and gather the key performance data and achieve the associated benefits of openly reporting group social and economic performance.

The communication approach was "top down" as commitment for sustainable development was from the chairman and appointed sustainable development

steering group representatives. Sub-committees were set up within each company and the policy was distributed to all operations directors in 1999.

Towards the end of 2000, data collection was coordinated through the Laing Technology Group Environmental Services. A communication committee was established that promoted internal communications over the intranet and internal journals. Various training programmes were developed for bidding, risk, health and safety, quality, project managers and supervisors.

Improved communication was also established through the project risk management system for assessing impacts and the quality management system for supply chain management and documentation. Communication also cross-linked to health and safety for auditing and emergency preparedness. This way the group could share the data that other systems produced. Existing procedures could be altered to include social and environmental considerations along with traditional assessments against cost, programme, risk, quality, technology and safety. New lines of communication were opened up more easily as data owners recognised the linkages and avoidance of duplication of work.

Communication also relied upon identifying other sustainable development champions within the group. Increased inter-divisional communication was also driven by peer pressure, the desire to be empowered and be part of the bigger sustainable construction performance initiative. Gradually more people wanted to play their part in the performance report.

The collection of data in itself formed a communication structure and understanding across departments for more openness. This improved communication and exposed strengths and gaps in data. The gaps indicated areas for improvement. This knowledge could then be used in future strategy planning to improve control in certain areas of the business for economic, social and environmental gain.

The benefits and lessons learned

- The performance results were published in the first and final web-based sustainability report in the millennium year. The most immediate benefit was the availability of the supporting performance data and "the ease and speed with which sustainability questions within the tender bidding process could be dealt with".

- There was a one-point source of information and case studies. There was no need for wasteful research and duplication of work. This information was immediately put to good use in the prime contracting process where, in some cases, up to 11 per cent of the tender score could be awarded for evidence of sustainable development policy and practice.

- The "bottom line" was that the use of corporate performance indicators could help secure long-term multi-million pound projects sustaining operations over periods of decades.

- Social and environmental reporting identified strengths and weaknesses in commercial business management. For example, gaps in data identified a need for greater control over supply chain management expenditure and utility bill anomalies.

- There was an improved capability to alter future strategies and respond to sustainable construction responsibilities.

- The raised awareness of building "sustainable structures in a sustainable way" was another step towards "lean construction" and more profitable projects.

- It meant improved site safety, environmental protection, loss prevention and conservation of resources resulting in improved eco-efficiency.

- The group enjoyed a two year period of increased environmental management control and "considerate construction" resulting in no convictions and associated costs or loss of time and resource.

- The group had provided evidence of sustainability policy, management and of "publicly reported performance" to qualify for the FTSE4 Good. From this would come the potential benefits of reduced insurance premiums and improved regulator confidence.

- This made the group more "investor friendly" and secured the potential to attract future ethical investment funds.

John Laing plc had taken another step towards becoming a more sustainable company with the business process, end product, local community, future stakeholders and surrounding environment benefiting. All of these improvements were driven, in some part, by the CIRIA sustainability indicators. The CIRIA Pioneers' Club had allowed the group to share its experiences of the external pressure and challenges. It had also facilitated feedback on how the challenges were being met in similar organisations.

The sharing of knowledge on measuring sustainable development accelerated the rapid learning that would have taken longer to acquire through a sole company initiative.

case study six

case study six

Establishing a system for selecting appropriate sustainable construction indicators

Company snapshot

Company:	*MWH*
Operations:	*Planning, engineering design, consultancy, construction and programme management.*
Sectors:	*Utility infrastructure, water treatment and supply, dams and reservoirs, wastewater treatment, drainage, utility infrastructure, pollution control, waste & power technologies*
Size:	*1580 staff in UK*
Turnover:	*£112 m (UK 2002)*
Major clients:	*UK water utility companies and multi-national industries*

Case study theme

The selection of sustainable construction indicators is an important step to measuring and reporting performance. This case study describes how MWH selected indicators for piloting. It also discusses how the work with Pioneers' Club has contributed to MWH's first sustainable development report and the lessons learned in selecting indicators for future reporting.

Corbett Challenge 2002. MWH fielded 15 teams to join in this challenge to climb the 111 peaks above 2500 ft in England and Wales. The teams were successful in raising about £4000 for Water Aid.

The build up to indicator adoption

In the UK, MWH's engagement with sustainable development has grown steadily over the last six years. This has been driven partly by the interest and increasing commitment of MWH staff, and partly as a supply-chain response to increased demands and interest from major clients. The "time line" box (Figure 1) shows the linked strands of that development, from 1999 to date. From the initial commitment to an environmental policy and adoption of an environmental management system (EMS) conforming to the requirements of ISO 14001, MWH has also begun to take a wider interest in the social and economic aspects of sustainable development.

The company facilitates a comprehensive range of services for clients, including:

- programme management
- asset management
- construction
- planning
- site assessment
- technology development
- plant design

Every one of these projects adds to "development" and every one of them makes the overall impact of development either more or less sustainable.

While the impacts of its own offices' performance on sustainable development is important, it is the performance of MWH projects for clients, that has a much bigger overall impact on sustainable development. Hence company policy on sustainable development is to focus first on its main operations and embed it – within its strategy and business practice – and then to report and account for it. To be able to measure and report on the progress of this policy, MWH has been investigating and testing a range of indicators for sustainable development, seeking key performance indicators (KPIs) that are appropriate to the company's business in the construction and water sectors.

This led to the company's involvement in the CIRIA Project to develop KPIs and to joining the Pioneers' Club.

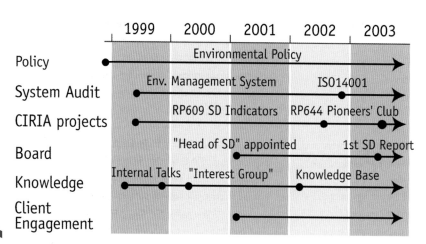

Figure 1 *The emergence of sustainable development initiatives within MWH*

How the indicators were selected to support sustainability

CIRIA's project *Sustainable Construction: Targets and Indicators*, identified a long list of KPIs that might be used to measure sustainable construction performance. The aim of the Pioneers' Club project was for member companies to test a selection of these in practice.

The initial project classed the indicators as either strategic or operational under the headings of environmental, social and economic. The Pioneers' Club only considered environmental and social indicators and CIRIA suggested 77 possible KPIs covering the environmental and social aspects of construction.

The first step in selecting KPIs for MWH was to draw up a list of the possible indicators identified in the initial project. This summary list included comments about how the KPIs might be applied to MWH and the existing systems that could be used or adapted for data collection.

To reduce the list to a manageable number of indicators relevant to MWH, the possible KPIs were assessed against a series of criteria. These criteria are explained in Figure 2.

EMS target	Does the CIRIA KPI match one of the targets in the MWH 2002 EMS?	
	Y	Yes
	N	No
Company or project level	Will the data for this indicator be collected at company or project level?	
	C	Company
	P	Project
Difficulty in collecting data	Measure of whether data and/or systems exist	
	1	Easy – existing data and systems
	2	Medium – either data or system are missing
	3	Hard – neither data nor system exist
Client influence	Is the performance of MWH on this indicator likely to be affected by client decisions at project or programme level?	
	Y	Yes
	N	No
Internal or external	This refers to the distinction between a sustainable company (Internal effects) and the effect of MWH's projects on the world (External)	
	I	Internal
	E	External
General relevance	Is this indicator relevant to MWH's activities?	
	1	Applies across company
	2	Applies on many projects
	3	Only limited relevance to MWH work

Figure 2 *Criteria against which indicators were assessed by MWH*

Having assessed the indicators against the criteria, the selection of KPIs for use in the Pioneers' Club was still a subjective process. The following general approach was adopted to make the final choice about whether the indicator should be adopted:

If an indicator is required to meet a target of the MWH EMS it has been selected. However, there are several aspects of the EMS (e.g. paper consumption) that are not included in the CIRIA KPIs.

The three either/ or criteria above namely:

● company/ project level

● client influence yes/ no

● internal/external,

have had little influence in selecting indicators. However, they do say something about the nature of the KPI and may be important when organising indicators for reporting purposes and in explaining performance.

Most weight has been given to the combination of difficulty and relevance assessed for each KPI.

The way in which combinations have been judged is shown in Figure 3 (1=high for relevance but low for difficulty).

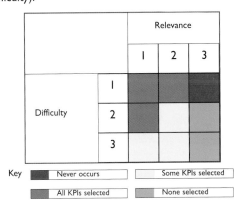

Key
| | Never occurs | | Some KPIs selected |
| | All KPIs selected | | None selected |

Figure 3 *Assessment of combinations of difficulty and relevance*

● Thus, if it is easy to collect data for a KPI (scores 1) and the indicator is widely relevant (scores 1), it has always been adopted.

● Similarly, if a KPI is either easy to collect (scores 1) and of medium relevance (scores 2) or is widely relevant (scores 1) and is fairly difficult to collect (scores 2) it has been selected.

● If the indicator is of little relevance (and is either difficult or fairly difficult to collect,) it has not been adopted.

For intermediate categories, indicators were selected on merit. Factors that favoured selection were:

● the KPI measures performance in an area identified as a priority for sustainable development within MWH

● it fills a gap where indicators would otherwise be lacking

● if data collection is considered medium hard (scores 2), at least the system exists.

A few KPIs were selected even though data collection was expected to be difficult. This was because the indicators were considered relevant to all or an important group of company activities and the indicator was aligned with a priority area for sustainable development. The two priority areas supported in this way were stakeholder engagement and energy saving on projects.

The result of this exercise was that MWH adopted the 25 environmental and social indicators shown in Figure 5 for the Pioneers' Club project.

The challenge of implementation across the company

The company is organised into the three main regional operating units of the Europe, Middle East, Africa and India (EMEAI), Asia, Australia and New Zealand (AANZ) and Americas. Within the EMEAI region, work is divided between UK operations and International country operations which is responsible for work outside the UK. The global and regional organisation are shown in Figure 4.

case study seven

UK operations comprise MWH UK Ltd and MWH Programme Management Ltd and work is carried out from the 11 main offices listed in Figure 4. With the exception of Inverness and the Isle of Man, these are the offices where MWH's EMS has been certified to ISO 14001. The 11 UK offices form the focus of the trial of CIRIA sustainable construction indicators. Work in joint venture with clients and constructors is also carried out from other project offices in the UK and although many of the company KPIs apply to MWH staff in these locations, it has not generally been possible to apply the operational KPIs in these offices.

An important initiative that has been progressed in coordination with the Pioneers' Club activities has been to report on MWH's sustainable development performance in the UK for 2002. The need to report to the Pioneers' Club and for reporting on

performance of the company EMS were among the reasons for deciding to produce a publicly available sustainable development report.

Preparing this report has engaged a wider group of senior managers within MWH than was involved with the Pioneers' Club project and has helped promote the ideas of sustainable development within MWH in the UK. By including a statement from the President of the MWH EMEAI Region and by publishing the report on the company's global website, awareness of the sustainable development performance and intentions of MWH in the UK has also been raised more generally across the global company.

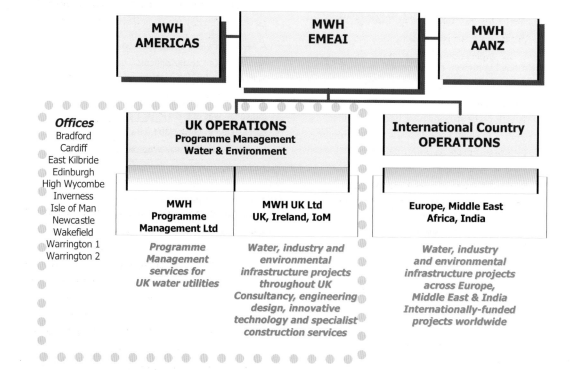

Offices
Bradford
Cardiff
East Kilbride
Edinburgh
High Wycombe
Inverness
Isle of Man
Newcastle
Wakefield
Warrington 1
Warrington 2

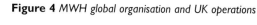

Figure 4 *MWH global organisation and UK operations*

Managing the process

The Pioneers' Club project, the EMS accreditation, and increased client interest, have together raised the profile of sustainable development within MWH. Sustainable indicator selection has contributed to other initiatives such as:

- identification and training of environmental champions and reviewers with responsibility for office and project activities respectively

- development of a global sustainable development knowledge community as part of MWH's knowledge management system

- actions with clients to encourage the use of more sustainable approaches at project level

- evaluation of energy savings through novel processes/designs to assess the scope for wider application of these approaches

- reporting on the sustainable development performance of MWH in the UK in 2002 as described above

- support of projects with MSc students looking at simple methods of evaluating whole-life costs of construction materials and introducing sustainability into designs.

The indicators selected for piloting

The selection of the indicators shown in Figure 5 was finalised in early 2002 as part of agreeing MWH's bespoke programme for the Pioneers' Club with CIRIA. A key development during 2002 was the decision to produce a sustainable development report for MWH in the UK. This initiative to produce a sustainable development report for MWH in the UK has run alongside the Pioneers' Club and has used data collected for the project.

To make the SD report as transparent and inclusive as possible, it was decided to follow the guidelines produced by the Global Reporting Initiative (GRI)

which offers one of the leading internationally recognised reporting systems. The GRI guidelines provide a reporting structure and a series of KPIs covering social, environmental and economic aspects. The GRI indicators are more wide ranging and less specific to construction than the CIRIA KPIs although many indicators are common to both GRI and CIRIA.

Figure 5 shows the GRI equivalent to the CIRIA KPI where one exists. Several of the CIRIA KPIs do not have a single equivalent GRI indicator, although related information may be collected under more than one GRI heading.

A summary of the reported results is given in Figure 5 and the full details are given in MWH's *UK Sustainable Development Report for 2002* which is available at
http://www.mwhglobal.com/sustDevReport.asp

In the SD report, the extent of MWH's compliance in reporting to the GRI guidelines has been marked by colour coding against each indicator using the following system:

NA	not applicable to MWH's UK business
	fully responsive
	partially responsive
	not responsive
C	confidential information

The same coding has been used in Figure 5.

In collecting information for the selected CIRIA KPIs it became evident that existing data collection systems were not able to provide comprehensive or quantified data to enable several of the indicators to be reported fully. For example, MWH currently has no central system to capture details of the standards of environmental performance or social engagement that have been agreed with clients. This information is known on some projects and such examples have been included in the SD report as a series of case histories as shown in Figure 5.

The comparison of the CIRIA and GRI KPIs has highlighted the importance of having an agreed set of standard measurements that can be applied across a sector.

This issue features as one of the talking points in MWH's 2002 SD Report. The CIRIA KPIs are a valuable contribution to the subset of indicators for the construction sector.

MWH is committed to a further report on its sustainable development performance in 2003 and data collection for this is ongoing. The reporting requirements for 2003 are currently being reviewed but, drawing on the experience of the 2002 report, it is likely that a more selective approach will be taken. This will focus on the aspects and indicators that are considered most relevant to MWH's business and align with the targets set for the EMS.

The starting point for the selection of appropriate indicators will be the system described in this case study.

This process is expected to lead to recognition that some GRI indicators are of less importance for MWH and to the adoption of additional indicators including some of those selected for piloting with the Pioneers' Club. Further work is needed within MWH to establish how reporting on some of the construction specific CIRIA KPIs can be made more comprehensive so as to move from case histories to full reporting.

	Indicator	GRI indicator	Result reported
	STRATEGIC – environmental		
1	% turnover of company operations with a formal or independently certified EMS to ISO 14001 or equivalent	❑	100%
2	% of projects for which environmental assessment has been undertaken and proposed environmental mitigation measures implemented	EN6,7,14 & 26	Case histories
3	Number of formal environmental or nuisance notices served due to construction activities	EN16	None
4	% of projects for which standards of environmental performance and social engagement have been formally agreed with the client	❑	Case Histories
5	% of projects for which whole-life costs and/or Life Cycle Assessment have been calculated and used in the design of the project or in the method of construction and materials used	❑	Case Histories
	STRATEGIC – social		
6	% of annual staff turnover for permanent staff	LA2	12.1%
7	Reportable fatal and non-fatal accidents per 100 000 hours worked	LA7	Two non-fatal reportable accidents in 2002
8	% of projects that include (and implement) a plan for stakeholder dialogue	❑	Case Histories
9	% of appropriate projects that include (and implement) a plan to consult with the end user	❑	Case Histories
10	% of turnover generated by projects undertaken under alliances or other forms of partnership working	❑	Not reported
	OPERATIONAL – environmental		
11	% of projects including: traffic management schemes during construction and use; dust control; noise controls; measures to prevent ground contamination; measures to prevent water contamination	❑	Case Histories
12	% of project sites for which an assessment of existing biodiversity has been undertaken prior to design and appropriate mitigation measures implemented	❑	Case Histories
13	CO_2 emitted per £ turnover	Office energy use reported under EN3	1.9 Million kWh of energy
14	% of energy demand by structures provided from: renewable resources, combined heat and power	❑	Case Histories
	OPERATIONAL – social		
15	% of staff receiving formal annual appraisals	EMP 5.1	100%
16	% of staff time used for giving or receiving formal training including social and environmental aspects of construction	LA9	Average of 23 hours per head
17	% of staff with a pension to which the company contributes	❑	71%
18	% of part time workers	LA1	4%
19	% of staff working more than 48 hours per week	❑	Not reported
20	% of employees declining offers of employment	❑	Not reported
21	Proportion of women employed	LA1	21%????
22	Proportion of women in senior management positions	❑	Not reported
23	% of eligible staff taking up share-save or similar schemes	❑	Not reported
24	% of company owned by employees	❑	100%
25	Value of charitable donation in money or time as a proportion of profits	EC10	£36,000

Figure 5 *Results for KPIs selected for piloting*

The benefits and lessons learned

MWH's main aims in joining the Pioneers' Club were:

- to share experience and knowledge

- translate issues into indicators

- set up a programme with targets.

The intention was that the Pioneers' Club would raise awareness and encourage sustainable approaches in pursuit of the longer term aims of:

- obtaining a better focus on how to apply the principles of sustainable development at both corporate and project level

- integrating sustainable development aims and practices into existing systems

- being among the construction industry leaders in practising sustainable development

The main beneficial lessons learned from the Pioneers' Club experience in relation to selecting and measuring KPIs have been:

- making full use of data held in existing management systems

- the aggregation of project level data to give the company wide operational or strategic indicators required

- the refining of several indicators to suit MWH activities and systems

- using available historic data to facilitate data collection and tracking of intra-company trends

- a clearer understanding of the difficulties in collecting comprehensive data from projects for operational indicators or to combine to form strategic indicators

- the realisation that the Pioneers' Club activities overlap with and help support several other sustainable development initiatives within MWH.

case study seven

case study seven

CIRIA

SKANSKA

Winning work by demonstrating sustainability performance

Company snapshot

Company:	*Skanska UK*
Operations:	*Infrastructure contracting – civil engineering, building, PFI, gas, mining, M&E, building services, ground engineering*
Sectors:	*Highways, Rail, Water, Commercial, Retail, Oil & Gas*
Size:	*4500 employees*
Turnover:	*£1.1 billion (2002)*
Major clients:	*NHS, Defence Estates, Highways Agency, Anglian Water, Network Rail*

Case study theme

This case study looks at how an awareness of emerging client demands for sustainability performance led Skanska into a fuller engagement with sustainable practices. Initial awareness resulted in the development of internal support for sustainability and the identification of the significant issues for the company.

Assessment and trialling of suitable indicators then followed. Building on its growing knowledge the company further investigated public procurement demands by carrying out research into key public sector policy documents. It was then possible to take data on performance, which was collected from the indicator implementation process, and feed it into tenders in a focussed way that addressed client conditions.

Barriers to the common application of indicators at project level became clear at an early stage. Skanska therefore has adopted an approach of responding to specific client needs by using indicators that are project specific.

Coventry Hospital main entrance

The build up to indicator adoption

- Skanska participated in the previous CIRIA project that devised the set of sustainability indicators for the construction industry

- Skanska realised that managing environmental issues alone was not sufficient for the future of the company or industry

- Issues relating to "Respect for People" were also being raised as key issues for the sustainability of the company

- Skanska's parent company (Skanska AB), always required annual reports on how environmental issues were being managed. In 2001 it was decided that for 2002 the company would produce a "sustainability report" and therefore certain high level sustainability indicators would be reported.

Skanska 2002 Sustainability Report

The use of performance indicators has been common in project management within the construction industry. However indicator use has been limited to production issues, cost forecasting, safety and, increasingly, environmental issues. To know which sustainability issues Skanska was managing well was difficult, as the company did not centrally collect the relevant data. Therefore the use of sustainability indicators through the Pioneers' Club provided the opportunity to tackle the subject.

Skanska's original intention was to gather data and benchmark its present position, particularly with regards to the corporate indicators, before setting improvement targets. However because winning work is such a key element for the business Skanska believed that it should firstly better understand the major sustainability issues of its clients. If it could demonstrate that it understood these issues, and had addressed them and, through the use of KPIs, measure achievement, then this would provide an advantage in winning work.

To do this the company invested time and resources to research the issues and propose a way forward. One outcome of this process was that the "project environment plan" was included within a broader based "sustainability plan", which included all the relevant objectives, targets and indicators.

Original selection of indicators

At the beginning of the Pioneers' Club project Skanska identified from the CIRIA list a number of environmental and social indicators for use. The criteria for choosing the indicators was challenging. They needed to be credible, practicable, useful and easily defined. All the environmental and social indicators needed to be useful to aid decision making and they also had to have a credibility that would promote their continued use.

The ease with which data could be consistently and accurately collected without imposing unacceptable bureaucracy on the business and project teams was paramount. Therefore the company tried to choose only those indicators where data already existed or where it believed data could be collected without undue paperwork.

Following a review of the selected indicators it was clear the environmental and social indicators identified were all at corporate level. Skanska believed that the aggregation of data from individual projects through its operating units to Skanska group level was not practicable at present. The prevailing circumstances at project level were so different that comparison or aggregation was not meaningful.

At the same time as discussions were being held within Skanska in the UK, Skanska AB (the parent company) issued a schedule of high level sustainability indicators (environmental and social) that it wished to collect as part of the 2002 *Sustainability Report*. Some of these indicators coincided with those on the CIRIA list.

From 2002 Skanska began to collect data for the strategic level social and environmental indicators for the Skanska *2002 Sustainability Report*.
It concluded that operational sustainability indicators should be developed at project level, so that they

were relevant and meaningful to the people collecting, collating and analysing the data. These would not be aggregated up through the organisation. Skanska has found this to be a more useful approach.

Strategic	
Environmental	**Social**
<ul><li>percentage of net sales covered by certified EMS</li><li>number of suppliers and subcontractors with certified EMS</li><li>number of internal and external audits undertaken</li><li>number of construction materials that have been environmentally assessed</li><li>percentage of projects where waste is separated into at least three waste streams</li></ul>	<ul><li>number of suppliers with whom long term alliances have been formed</li><li>percentage of staff on structured training programmes</li><li>percentage of staff receiving annual appraisals.</li><li>number of RIDDOR reportable accidents</li><li>number of employees participating in specialist training.</li></ul>

Figure 1 *Examples of Skanska strategic environmental and social indicators.*

How the indicators support sustainability

At project level Skanska wanted its sustainability indicators to show how well it was meeting the objectives it had set to meet the requirements and commitments of its client and the business in general.

When working for government clients the company considered an extensive range of documents from central government, local government and the procuring government department.

Central government has explained how it will meet its commitment to sustainable development through publications such as:

- *Greening Government*

- *A Better Quality of Life: a strategy for sustainable development for the UK*

- *Achieving Sustainability in Construction Procurement*, Sustainability Action Group Government's construction Clients Panel (GCCP) June 2000

The document *Achieving Sustainability in Construction Procurement* sets objectives for the end of March 2003, for all government departments and requires:

- that procurement will be in line with value for money on the basis of whole life costs

- that there are targets for energy and water consumption for new projects that contribute significantly to the achievement of cross-government targets agreed by "Green" ministers

- protection of habitat and species

- an increase in the number of construction projects achieving "excellent" under the BREEAM (or NEAT) assessment schemes

Similarly, there are other publications that impact upon individual spending departments. These include:

- *Sustainable Development for the NHS* (2001)

This document highlights how the sustainability of the NHS can be increased through its estate management (planning, design and construction, operation, purchasing and supply and partnership)

- *Framework for sustainable development on the Government Estate* (2002)

- *New Environmental Strategy for NHS* (2002).

Again these strategies set objectives, targets and in some cases specify key indicators.

When all these strategies and policy statements are put together with the requirements of Local Agenda 21, (which outlines how local authorities are to promote and achieve sustainability in their areas), you have a host of commitments that a potential client has made.

Atrium at New Coventry Hospital

Skanska takes the view that it is part of its remit to help the client achieve its commitments by designing its construction projects to fulfil client goals.

For example, if a client sets targets for energy use or for the creation of new habitat on its new projects or its existing building stock, then Skanska will develop its objectives, targets and indicators to show how it will assist the client to meet or exceed its expectations.

Examples of this are:

- energy targets of GJ/100 m³ of building space per annum

- water usage of m³/bed-space per annum

- a target rate for procurement of services from companies in the local area

- to conduct formal sustainability audits during design, construction and operation phases.

As stated earlier the operational indicators will vary between projects. These are developed from the project objectives. Skanska identifies indicators for each objective and defines how the data will be collected and handled to ensure it is accurate and consistent.

Typical objectives for PFI projects include targets addressing:

- operating an ISO 14001 environmental management system

- conducting environment risk assessment for all construction activities

- procurement issues relating to materials and subcontractors

- management of waste

- urban renewal

- noise and nuisance.

Kings College Hospital

The company believes that, by setting and achieving these sustainability objectives (as measured by sustainability indicators), it will deliver better value for money and produce savings on energy, waste, water usage and natural resources both during construction and when the buildings are in use.

This is a way of demonstrating the company's commitment to sustainable development.

The challenge of implementation across the group

Environmental management activity is supported both at group level in the UK, at operating unit level and at project level, by a team of qualified environmental managers.

Each operating unit within the Skanska UK Construction Group operates a certified EMS to ISO 14001, and hence has a systematic formal approach to identifying and managing environmental impacts that arise from it's work. Each project has a project specific environmental plan, which identifies the key environmental impacts, the controls and any key performance indicators. Skanska's major projects are now replacing the environment plan with a sustainability plan. The sustainability plan addresses a wider range of issues looking at social impacts and social KPIs, in addition to the environmental issues.

Skanska is now beginning to understand what the "sustainability indicators" are telling the business about how well it manages the issues.

In future the company will use operational indicators that are specific to the project. Although it may use the same indicators on more than one project it does not intend, at this stage, to aggregate them. Skanska will also use strategic sustainability indicators which will be owned by the operating unit.

Skanska is a large and complex organisation. It believes its operating units that act as "principal contractors" have the greatest pressure to address sustainability in construction. They are also best placed to deal with them, having the necessary skills and resources available and the ability to call upon specialist support as required. The group's smaller specialist businesses are not subject to the same drivers and although they are managing many of the same issues they are not encompassing them in an explicitly "sustainable construction" format.

Managing the process

At each stage of the process, from tender through construction to operations, a Skanska environment manager or adviser is used as overseer. At tender stage the environment manager will work closely with the design team to decide the objectives and targets needed for the project, and to ascribe appropriate indicators to measure progress.

During the construction phase a dedicated member of the EHS team on site will collate and forward the data on the sustainability indicators to the business management team. This forms part of the operating unit report papers.

As the number of projects reporting against project sustainability indicators increases there is the option to establish a steering group to review progress, the appropriateness of the objectives and indicators and what improvement can be made, as well as the exchange of best practice.

Benefits and lessons learned

Skanska sees clear benefits from using sustainability indicators as part of the work-winning strategy. The company believes that clients that procure contractors by their ability to meet given sustainable construction criteria, and then measure the contractors progress by the use of sustainability indicators, will get better value for money.

At present not all clients, including government clients, use sustainability indicators as a tool to assess the ability of their contractors. If clients do ask for specific indicators, these are often limited to the management of environmental issues.

case study eight

By using sustainability indicators clients will achieve the following benefits:

- they will know if they are meeting their own long and medium-term objectives

- they will be able to differentiate between the good contractor and the excellent one

- they will show that they are serious in addressing the issues associated with sustainable development

- contractors will develop a detailed understanding of the client requirements. They can therefore plan for the future by developing the skills needed and invest in training and development of their people.

Skanska has learned a number of lessons from trialling sustainable construction in indicators:

- performance indicators need to be practicable, credible and useful

- operational data is difficult to collect and aggregate, and not consistent enough to be used at corporate level

- all indicators have some problems in being easily and clearly defined. There are also problems in finding an appropriate and useful normalisation base.

- until the definition is clear and the boundaries set for the collection of data there will always be a question of accuracy

- the use of environmental and social indicators at project level has helped focus attention on important issues

- where clients have clearly stated what their objectives are Skanska is able to help them by using appropriate indicators

- clients that do use sustainability indicators get better value for money over the project life.

Some brief examples of how Skanska UK intends to develop indicator initiatives

- extend the use of the "sustainability plans" for major projects in all business streams

- benchmark performance using the information gathered from existing projects

- introduce new indicators to assist decision making on future projects and remove those indicators that are not adding value

- promote the use of key sustainability indicators with those clients that do not already require them

- set up a forum to review the use of Sustainability Indicators to date and decide on future strategy.

Taylor Woodrow

Construction waste measurement within an environmental management system – how detailed data changed behaviour

Company snapshot

Company:	*Taylor Woodrow Construction*
Operations:	*Capital project delivery, Engineering and technology consultancy, , facilities and asset management, project finance*
Sectors:	*Retail, transport, residential*
Size:	*1650 UK employees*
Turnover:	*£450 m per annum*
Major clients:	*Tesco, BAA, Shell,*

Case study theme

Implementing sustainable construction practices sometimes involves "picking the low hanging fruit first". TWC found that early progress could be made by linking its work with indicators to the development of its Environmental Management System (EMS), particularly given the ISO 14001 requirement to be audited on continual improvement.

Although social sustainability indicators were equally important to the company they proved to have longer gestation periods in terms of putting in place the required data management and culture change plans. In contrast environmental management was an area that has yielded relatively rapid performance improvement benefits and developing this aspect, has helped build confidence in sustainability performance measurement and data reporting generally. Within this context the following aspects have received particular focus:

- waste
- water pollution prevention
- "nuisance" – noise and dust
- materials selection/sustainable timber
- CO_2 emissions.

"Getting on and doing" as opposed to building up the

sustainability framework in a "top down" and theoretical manner was important in selling key messages back to senior management who needed to see evidence of commercial benefits. An excellent starting point is waste minimisation – achieving successes in this area provides a good morale boost for supporting sustainability generally and direct financial gains.

The challenges of sustainable waste management exposes issues which get to the heart of the industry's problem with tracking and improving performance generally: multiple projects; varying timescales; diversity of sectors and client demands; range of materials; changing locations; site space constraints; health & safety issues; and different workforces. The learning experiences were therefore invaluable.

The build up to indicator adoption

The figure below shows the path TWC has taken. This has recently culminated in the company moving beyond "compliance" to a broader engagement with sustainability.

⊃ A range of systems had been in place for a number of years with TWC achieving a very good track record in pollution prevention.

⊃ The Business Excellence Model (BEM) was providing a degree of relevant experience of measuring performance in key areas.

⊃ Partnering with customers and suppliers was recognised as leading to benefits for clients in terms of quality and cost certainty

⊃ A number of recent industry awards to TWC served as reminders of the benefits from innovation and continual improvement.

⊃ The EMS process began in February 2001. Site visits, project team briefings (to 190 staff) and a mentoring programme commenced.

⊃ EMS communications were established through email and "Tayweb", the Taylor Woodrow intranet.

⊃ Safety, Health & Environment (SHE) site inspections were implemented, providing aggregated 6 monthly scores across 15 project aspects based on detailed questionnaires. Targets are linked to staff bonuses.

⊃ Focus on sustainable waste management.

Figure 1 *Steps in engagement with sustainability*

SHE site inspections

The 15 project aspects measured in the SHE site inspections
1   Administration.
2   Fire protection/prevention.
3   Working platforms.
4   Work places.
5   Mobile plant & equipment.
6   Other requirements/ regulations.
7   PPE.
8   Access.
9   Health & welfare.
10 Housekeeping.
11 Public protection.
12 Training & information.
13 Emergency/permit procedures.
14 Environmental/community.
15 Product specific.

The 15 aspects of the SHE site inspections Jan – June 2002 are measured for each project (represented by a blue bar) and aggregated into one overall score table

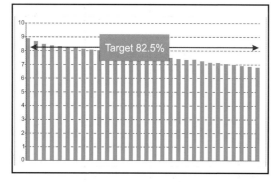

Target 82.5%

How the indicators support sustainability

During the assessment and trialling of indicators TWC sought to understand how to collect meaningful detailed data at project level to inform management decisions about performance improvement strategies.

For the trialling process it primarily wanted to achieve better waste management as part of its EMS implementation – but it needed to do this in a manner which built general commitment and data management lessons applicable to other areas of sustainability. Where appropriate a transition towards formal industry benchmarking on key sustainability issues was envisaged.

There was a clear recognition that repeat business, which represented more than 75 per cent of the order book, was extremely important to the business. It was therefore essential to understand how to satisfy the requirements of the client.

Indicators and performance improvement processes had to take account of all stakeholder pressures – but particularly had to ensure that the right messages could be conveyed to the client.

Therefore a flow of quality information had to be facilitated in a form which would feed into transparent sustainability reporting.

Managing the data – learning from waste

Although the construction industry uses more than 400 m tonnes of resources per year and produces more than 90 m tonnes of waste, it has not been particularly successful in quantifying and minimising wastes at project level.

There are particular challenges around the interpretation of waste indicators across projects. And it is recognised within the industry that inter-company comparisons of waste performance is hampered by project diversity. However, waste is now gaining a higher profile within the industry and within TWC.

TWC started by assessing the scale of the problem by compiling broad historical information on disposal costs from past TWC construction operations. This was available from the "skip cost code" within the accounting system. Table 1 indicates direct waste disposal costs for TWC for the years 2000, 2001 and 2002.

Table 1 *Waste disposal costs for TWC*

2000		2001		2002	
Cost (£)	% of turnover	Cost (£)	% of turnover	Cost (£)	% of turnover
578,000	0.17	1,169,810	0.28	1,206,266	0.3

The figures revealed costs were significant and, given the low profit margins for most contracting work, disposal costs as a percentage of turnover were noteworthy. The figures also suggested potentially significant environmental impacts.

This broad information motivated the company to investigate further.

Faced with an absence of performance data on which to base improvement targets, the next stage was to attempt to compile meaningful detailed information so that performance could begin to be compared.

This proved challenging because of the severe time constraints on knowledge management activities within site teams. However, TWC was able to collect data on a range of projects, a selection of which are shown in Table 2.

Table 2 *Historical waste data for 11 projects*

1	2	3	4	5	6
Project	Description	Bulk Volume (m³)	Floor area (m²)	Bulk Vol/ floor area (m³/ 100m²) project cost	Cost of disposal as % of total (%)
Retail store	new store	997	6,435	15	0.25
Retail store	new store	1,414	9,012	16	0.39
Retail store	new store	1,600	9,445	17	0.36
Retail store	new store	2,476	8,972	28	0.21
Office – Philipshill Business Park	shell and core	908	5,343	17	0.20
Residential – GMV Phase 1A	excl. frame & excl. recycled materials	2,349	10,546	22	0.26
Residential – GMV Phase 1A	excl. frame but incl. recycled materials	2,859	10,546	27	0.30
Residential – Macintosh Village Phase B	concrete frame	2,436	5,500	44	0.5
Residential – Macintosh Village Phase A	load bearing masonry	2,021	3,466	58	0.56
Residential – Montevetro	excluding frame	9,135	10,000	91	–
Residential – TWC City Quays	phases 2–5	16,197	12,000	135	–

This more detailed information helped the company to understand how different types of projects resulted in different waste streams and disposal costs.

A project waste benchmark was used on Greenwich Millennium Village (a joint venture between Countryside Properties and Taylor Woodrow) which is discussed below. Waste monitoring activities were then initiated producing data for improvement targets. The process resulted in staff being encouraged to engage in performance improvement measures. The information highlighted several issues which then guided further improvement strategies:

➲ *An overall company figure for disposal costs is not useful for benchmarking purposes*

➲ *Information was not available on skips procured by subcontractors*

➲ *Project benchmarking is more viable than comparisons between years. and comparisons between companies is currently difficult*

➲ *The costs in Table 2 do not account for waste from earthworks activities which on some projects can be a significant waste stream*

➲ *Disposal costs do not reflect the true cost of waste. Including the cost of materials wasted, handling, re-work etc this is estimated to be approximately 7.5 times disposal costs (Ref. Construction, The Price of Waste. September 2000. DETR Partners in Innovation Project).*

For the Greenwich Millennium Village Project, TWC employed a waste management monitoring tool developed by BRE, SMARTWaste (Figure 2). The tool facilitates the collection of data on both waste quantities and waste types, as shown in Figure 3.

Figure 2 *BRE SMARTWaste tool*

Improvements driven by measurement on the GMV project

Working with external consultants, who used the quantification tool to continually monitor wastes arising, TWC developed and implemented management control procedures to respond to the incoming data and minimise the levels of waste generated during the construction process.

GMV has now moved on to another phase of development and the challenge is to improve upon the waste performance of Phase 1a. For this process the lessons that TWC will take from the first phase are as follows:

- raise awareness within the project team by using data to highlight quantities and reduction opportunities

- use pre-manufactured units where possible – pre-manufactured bathroom pods were used on Phase 1a

- use cladding systems (eg timber faced and render) for the exterior as opposed to brick and block

- manage skips well – care was taken to ensure that the skips were full and compacted before leaving site

- design is of crucial importance – in developing the design for the project the waste minimisation aspects that were considered were prefabrication, standardisation of components and modularisation

- once on site, construction teams are often limited by space

- there are challenges in terms of obtaining the buy-in to waste minimisation from subcontractors

- packaging is becoming the largest waste stream on construction sites and there appears to be only limited dialogue between major contractors at one end of the supply chain and materials manufacturers at the other end of the supply chain

- the availability of recycling capacity is a problem, particularly with respect to plastics and plasterboard.

Sustainable waste management tends to arise more where the client has an interest in the issue making it a higher priority for the site team.

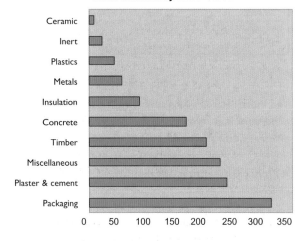

Figure 3 *Waste streams – GMV Phase 1 A*

Greenwich Millennium Village

Plasterboard success

A major success on site was segregation of plasterboard off-cuts for recycling. Detailed quantification showed that plasterboard waste accounted for 15 per cent of total waste on the project by volume.

Ordinarily, waste plasterboard from construction sites will end up in a landfill site. Plasterboard is a recyclable material but until recently there has been no drive for recycling or for improving the capability for recycling in the UK. A requirement to initiate minimisation of waste and to participate in recycling was incorporated into the subcontractor tender package. TWC worked closely with the subcontractor and British Gypsum, to successfully introduce the segregation scheme.

The result was that almost all the plasterboard waste (175 m³ – 87 per cent of plasterboard waste) was returned to British Gypsum for recycling.

Future projects

TWC is spreading good practice from GMV, one aspect of which is the introduction of the BRE SMARTStart waste monitoring tool on new projects.

To further support this process TWC has:

- expanded its environmental training programmes

- set up forums/networks to spread best practice

- developed a sustainability knowledge channel on Tayweb

- developed a waste management toolbox on Tayweb

- reviewed its waste management supply chain

- achieved commitment of the management team of TWC

In addition to other social and environment indicators being trialled, other relevant CIRIA resource-related indicators that TWC is currently assessing or is interested in looking at in the future are as follows:

Operational environmental

- percentage of secondary and recycled aggregate used in construction
- percentage of timber used in construction from well managed, sustainable sources
- average distance travelled per tonne of materials from suppliers to site (km)
- CO_2 released (in tonnes) per £ turnover arising from construction activities (DETR, 1999b)
- CO_2 released (in tonnes) per £ turnover (DETR, 1999b) arising from business related non-site activities

Note

Obtaining waste quantities in tonnes, as per the CIRIA indicator, "Tonnes of wastes arising to landfill per £ turnover" was not possible at this stage as past records provided only volume-based information.

case study nine

Core values and KPIs

Introduction

This case study describes the process of development and the challenges faced in the introduction of a performance measurement system for the UK business.

The case for sustainable development

Background to WSP

WSP Group plc is a global business providing management and consultancy services to the built and natural environment. Established in 1969, WSP was listed on the London Stock Exchange in 1987 and through strategic development, the company has grown into one of the largest international consultancy groups in the world. In brief the company has:

- more than 4500 staff operating out of 110 offices worldwide (corporate HQ in London, UK)

- a projected annualised turnover of £300 million

- received 40% income from UK and 60% from overseas

- multi-disciplinary planning, engineering, environmental and management skills and is active in the building, environmental, management consultancy, transport & utility infrastructure fields of activity

- a full range of service from planning, through to studies, design, implementation and maintenance

- completed major projects worldwide, drawing upon the capability of five prime divisions: management consultancy, environmental, property, transport & utility infrastructure

WSP's Core Values

WSP's vision is "To be the preferred choice supplier of our professional services within the built environment both in the United Kingdom and internationally." Supporting this vision are the company's five core values. They serve not only as goals for the company to achieve, but also define behaviours that teams and individuals are encouraged and expected to adopt.

Figure I *The drivers for sustainability in WSP*

The aim of a sustainable business is to maintain its performance against the changing needs of:

- its clients

- its shareholders

- its staff

- society

WSP is no different. However, there is increasing pressure for WSP to demonstrate this sustainability to these stakeholders; each has a vested interest in the performance of the business, albeit from different perspectives.

However, if you can't measure your performance how can you demonstrate it to others? More importantly, if you can't measure it, how can you <u>manage</u> it?

Measurement of performance is therefore the first step for any company (assuming it has a vision and strategy in place) in becoming a sustainable business.

Background to the review of performance measurement

At the start of 2002, the UK business reflected on its strategy of business improvement. High on the list of requirements was the need for a performance measurement system (for the purpose of clarity, the word "system" in this paper refers to the overall process, whether automated or not).

Up until this time, WSP had placed heavy emphasis on measuring business success on the "bottom-line" results. Non financial indicators were measured and reported on, but in many cases locally, inconsistently and in isolation of other indicators, particularly when dealing with the actioning of change. It is important to note that a number of initiatives leading up to 2002 had made significant strides in performance measurement – specifically the introduction of the employee survey (carried out annually since 2000) and the undertaking of a client survey in 2001. However, there was an increasing awareness and understanding among senior management of the UK business, of the need for a more balanced method of measuring business performance, and one that in particular recognised influencing factors of certain measures over others.

The requirements for a performance measurement were outlined by the UK executive committee early in 2002 as follows:

- the effort required to measure the business's performance should not be excessive or become a burden (should become part of the "day job")

- it must be possible to analyse/compare the performance of each operating company as well as that of the UK Business as a whole

- it should support and re-enforce the WSP core values

- it must be kept simple

- the output must be in a form that is communicable to the stakeholders listed earlier.

So with these in mind, a project to establish KPIs for the UK, was born.

The sustainability challenge

The options

From the start of the project, there were two clear options on the way forward for a WSP UK performance measurement system; to adopt an established "off-the-shelf", externally recognised framework (ie the Business Excellence Model or Balanced Scorecard), or to develop an in-house solution.

Of all of the externally recognised frameworks, the Business Excellence Model (BEM) was the most well known within WSP. At the time, WSP's Civils (in response to the strategy of its public sector clients the Highways Agency and Strategic Rail Authority) had begun to introduce the BEM as a means of measuring their business performance. However, there was a reluctance to introduce this at UK level until it had been piloted. Additionally, the team was aware of the Construction Best Practice (CBPP) KPIs. These were reviewed for their applicability, and concern was expressed at the appropriateness of these to WSP. In the short-term therefore, a simple in-house solution was deemed more appropriate.

There had already been a significant involvement from WSP in the CIRIA Pioneers' Club and the identification of potential indicators. Although more focused on environmental sustainability, this work formed the "kernel" of the development of the UK business KPIs.

Designing the system

The design of the performance measurement system is focused around the company's core values and is structured as follows:

- each core value has a number of KPIs allocated

Profitability
Productivity
Repeat business

Balanced Commercial Approach

Valued & Committed Employees

Training Delivered
Staff Turnover
Staff Absence
Productivity

Environmental Awareness

Excellent Client Service

Energy Usage

Repeat Business
Partnering/Framework
PII Claims

Innovation

Figure 2 *A mock-up of the output from the in-house solution*

Technical Papers Issued
Training Delivered

- the relationship between a KPI and a core value is mapped as direct, indirect or none

- the performance of each KPI against its pre-established target is reported using traffic light indicators

  – red indicating that performance is outside of established targets

  – amber indicating performance either inside or outside of established targets although the trend predicts a change next period

  – green indicating that performance is within target

- the performance of the core value is similarly measured by rolling up the results of the KPIs and a simple set of rules dictates how this works

- Some KPIs may be related to more than one core value

- reported quarterly – this is seen as the optimum balance between avoiding information overload and burden, and having timely and relevant data

- an Excel-based spreadsheet would be used to manage the collection and reporting of data

A mock-up of what was considered to be the end report is illustrated in Figure 2.

The challenges in establishing the system

Some key challenges emerged during the development of the performance measurement system, notably the current organisational structure of the UK business; the selection of the indicators; agreeing the relationship between the indicators and the core values; agreeing the targets for some of the indicators. It is fair to say that many of these challenges have not been resolved. Therefore, a trial period of six months (the first two quarters of 2003), has taken place in which the outputs have been kept within the UK Excom, to allow modifications to be made, and to get it as near as right as possible before communicating to a wider audience.

Selecting the indicators
At the outset, criteria were laid out for what constituted a successful indicator. Ideally, it was agreed, they must be:

- appropriate – a true indicator against a core vale or company strategy

- objective – if it can't easily be defined, don't measure it!

- accurate – only small margins of error in the data provided would be acceptable

- discriminating – small changes in data should be meaningful

- a leading indicator – allowing assumptions to be made about future trends

- collectable – easy, inexpensive and unobtrusive to collect

- benchmark-able – to seek out best practice

- quantifiable – easy to analyse.

Following the identification of more than 20 indicators at a brainstorming session of senior management, and on further analysis, it became apparent that many of the indicators simply wouldn't pass the criteria set. Only the financially-based indicators passed with flying colours; not wholly unexpected considering the business had traditionally placed a greater emphasis on financial reporting and with an established accounting system in place. This resulted in some of the core values (such as innovation and environmental awareness) being very poorly served indeed.

The main root causes of the failure of the indicators proposed are listed in the Appendix.

The organisational structure of the UK business

As a number of relatively autonomous operating companies within a UK business, performance measurement had been performed, and in most cases very successfully. However, with the exception of some of the commercial and financial KPIs, there was no real consistency in the definitions, methods of measurement, and no single source of data for the UK. This meant that consensus was required and many of the operating companies had to make changes to the way they collected their existing data.

Agreeing the relationship between the KPIs and the core values

Some KPIs clearly belonged to one core value only (such as "number of technical papers issued" with the "innovation" core value). For others, however, the relationships were greyer and there was difference of opinion about how directly certain indicators related to the core values. If one takes "training days per employee", there is the argument that, as an indicator, it relates directly to all of the core values – not just "valued & committed employees". The initial trial period will go a long way in understanding how best to map these relationships.

Agreeing targets for the KPIs

The issue of national benchmark results by organisations such as the Chartered Institute of Personnel Development (CIPD), and the annual business planning cycle within WSP UK, meant that many of the KPIs had their targets pre-set. However, there were a few of the indicators for which setting targets was more or less starting from scratch (eg "What is our target for repeat business?"). The risk is that the targets set are too ambitious and, quarter on quarter, all of the indicators are flashing red, sending out perhaps too negative a message to stakeholders. The trial period will be hugely important in making sure that the targets set are realistic.

The benefits of sustainable construction

At the time of writing, WSP is about to carry out its first session of reporting. It is the experience of the author that on many projects, the benefits that actually materialise are not the ones primarily set out to achieve. It will be interesting to see whether this is the case on this project. For the record however, the intended benefits fall into three main groupings:

1 **To support the management of the UK business**: As a balanced dashboard, the measurement would act as a "health check" and/or "early warning" system for the business, allowing more informed decision making by management within the business.

2 **To drive continuous improvement:** As a measurement tool, at both a strategic

and operational level, weaker areas would be highlighted, helping direct strategy and prioritise improvement projects. As important would be the ability to benchmark WSP's performance against external organisations, and so enabling best practice. Finally, it is often difficult to measure the impact of an initiative. With the introduction of this tool covering a range of indicators, these impacts could start to be assessed.

3 **Communication:** A major benefit of this tool will be its ability to communicate and clarify strategy to staff and shareholders, particularly when used on the company's intranet site.

Conclusion

It is important to understand the limitations of the system, in order to know how to enhance it in the future. To use an analogy... this system will provide our car with a dashboard of how efficiently we are driving the car (is the engine overheating?, how fast are we travelling?, how warm is it inside the car?); it does not tell us in which direction we are travelling and whether we are on course. It does not, therefore, provide us with an indication of performance against a specific UK strategy, as the principles of the Balanced Scorecard outline. It would not be difficult to integrate this into the system in the way that it is currently designed, and this is something to look at once the basic system is working successfully.

In 2003, the capability of the system as it stands already looks like being strengthened through a number of other projects taking place in within the UK business in that year. There is a proposal for an HRM system which, if implemented, would improve the robustness of the company's "people" data; property Management is being centralised within the UK, which would provide a central source of data related to indicators such as energy usage.; finally, the

introduction of key account management within the UK will provide the mechanism to obtain improved data about and from clients.

This project is a new concept for WSP at a UK level, and is certainly a reflection of the changing approach of the senior management. The project will benefit the business as much for the change in attitude towards performance measurement among management and staff alike, as it will for the actual output itself.

Appendix

- Training delivered
  - *Average no. of training days per permanent employee*
- Staff turnover
  - *Permanent employees leaving voluntarily as a % of total permanent employees*
- Staff absence (through sickness)
  - *Days lost to absence as a % of total days (for all staff)*
- Repeat business
  - *Value of work won as repeat business as a % of total work won*
- Proportion of order book that is partnering/ framework
  - *Value of order book that is within a partnering or framework agreement as a % of total order book.*
- Number of open claims (PII)
  - *The number of claims currently open against WSP*
- Insurer's reserve (PII)
  - *Insurer's reserve as a % of net turnover*
- HSE reported incidents
  - *The number of H&S incidents reported to the HSE per 1000 employees*
- Number of technical papers Issued
  - *The number of technical papers presented or published per 1000 employees*
- Profitability
- Return on capital employed
- Productivity.

case study ten

CIRIA

Appendix 3   CIRIA sustainable construction indicators chart

Government sustainability principles: Effective protection of the environment and prudent use of natural resources

Theme	Key issues	Sub-issues for Award Scheme criteria	d/c/g	Operational indicators (environmental and social)	d/c/g
Avoiding pollution	Measures implemented to avoid, mitigate and manage pollution from site	Has an EMS been implemented?	g	Percentage of projects per £ turnover including: ● Traffic management schemes during construction and use ● Dust control ● Noise controls ● Measures to prevent ground contamination ● Measures to prevent water contamination	d
		Is the EMS formally accredited to recognised standard? (eg ISO 14001 or EMAS)	g	Number of environmental or nuisance notices served due to construction activities per £ turnover	c
		Identification of potential pollution sources and design of mitigation measures	d	SO2, PM10 and NOx released (in tonnes) per £ turnover arising from construction activities	c
		Minimising polluting emissions on site	d	Number of complaints received per project site for noise and dust	c
		Effective site supervision (where consultant is employed in a client resident engineer capacity).	c	Proportion of construction costs on nuisance mitigation	c
		Preventing nuisance from noise and dust by good site management	c	See Strategic Indicators	
		Preventing pollution incidents and breaches of environmental legislation requirements	c		
Avoiding pollution and efficient use of natural resources	Transport planning	Greening fleet of company cars	g	Average distance travelled per tonne of materials from suppliers to site (km)	c
		Route planning	g		
		Car sharing	g		
		Percentage of public transport use for company business	g		
		Percentage of no-emission travel (cycling etc)	g		
		Development of green commuting plan	g		
		Minimising travel	g		
Protecting and enhancing biodiversity	Protecting existing species and enhancing biodiversity. AND Habitat and environmental improvement	Has an environmental appraisal been undertaken and environmental mitigation measures implemented?	g	Percentage of project sites for which an assessment of existing biodiversity has been undertaken before design and appropriate mitigation measures implemented	d
		Identification of opportunities to enhance biodiversity by habitat creation	d	Area of habitat designed and created	d
		Design-in environmental improvements such as by landscaping or habitat creation	d	Percentage of project sites for which appropriate mitigation measures have been implemented to protect sensitive ecosystems	c
		Specification of native species for planting/ seeding	d	Number of non-conformance certificates issued by £ turnover	c
		Protecting sensitive ecosystems through good design practices.	c	Cost of environmental improvements designed as a proportion of total project costs	d
		Planting of native species	c		
		Protecting sensitive ecosystems through good construction practices and supervision	c		
		Dealing with unforeseen protected / harmful species	c		
	Optimising use of brownfield sites	Using brownfield sites in favour of greenfield sites	d		
	Environmentally sensitive design and construction	Consideration of flora and fauna, landscape	g		
Improving energy efficiency and management	Designing for whole life costs	Energy efficient building design	d	Energy efficiency of the building design for domestic buildings – The average SAP rating for all dwellings designed	d
		Energy efficient construction processes	c	Energy efficiency of the building designs for non domestic buildings – Average % beyond building regulations (either for insulation levels of the building fabric or an overall energy target)	d
		Reduced energy consumption in business activities.	g	Percentage of relevant projects (by turnover) for which a BREEAM score (or similar system) been calculated	d
				Percentage of projects achieving an "excellent" rating using BREEAM (or similar system) for new construction projects	d
				Percentage of projects achieving an "excellent" rating using BREEAM (or similar system) for refurbishment projects	d
				CO2 released (in tonnes) per £ turnover arising from construction activities (DETR, 1999b)	c
				Percentage of projects (by turnover) for which the M4I index of project sustainability has been calculated. The average score of projects measured	d
				CO2 emitted per £ turnover (DETR, 1999b)	
Efficient use of resources	Use of local supplies & materials with low embodied energy	Incorporation of renewable energy sources or combined heat and power schemes into development design.	d	Percentage of energy demand by structure provided from: ● Renewable sources ● Combined heat and power	d
		Specify materials with low embodied energies	d	Percentage of projects (by turnover) incorporating renewable energy systems or combined heat and power	d
		Use of materials with low embodied energies	c		
	Waste minimisation management AND reuse of existing built assets	Design for whole-life costs and minimum waste in construction, use and afterlife.	d	Tonnes of wastes arising to landfill per £ turnover	c
		Waste management plan implemented	c	Tonnes of hazardous wastes arising per £ turnover	c
		Reusing materials, including those already on site, (where applicable through treatment)	c	Percentage of projects with a waste minimisation strategy	d
		Use recycled/reclaimed materials, or those from sustainable supplies	c	CO2 released (in ones) per £ turnover (DETR, 1999b) arising from business related non-site activities	c
				No generic indicators – sector specific indicators are more appropriate	
				Percentage of projects for which life-time costs have been derived and were a material considera-tion in the design	d
				Predicted treated water consumption for new buildings in litres per person per day (lppd) averaged over all projects of a similar type	d
				Design capacity of grey-water and rainfall collection systems	d
				Tonnes of unused construction materials disposed to landfill	c
				Percentage of materials intentionally over-ordered by value	c

Efficient use of resources (cont) / Effective protection of the environment and prudent use of natural resources (cont)

Key issues	Sub-issues for Award Scheme criteria	d - design c - construction g - generic	Operational indicators (environmental and social)	d - design c - construction g - generic
Use of reclaimed/ recycled/ sustainably-sourced products	Specify reclaimed/ recycled materials	d	Percentage of secondary and recycled aggregate used in construction	d
	Specify materials from sustainable supplies	d	Percentage of timber used in construction from well managed, sustainable sources	d
	Use of reclaimed/ recycled materials	c	Percentage of recycled and secondary aggregate used in construction	c
	Use of materials from sustainable supplies	c	Percentage of timber used in construction from well managed, sustainable sources	c
Lean design and construction	Designing and constructing using materials efficiency and effectively	g		
	Propose lean designs avoiding over-engineering	d		
	Lean construction avoiding waste	c		
Water conservation	Design to conserve water in use including, where appropriate, rainfall-capture and grey-water systems.	d		
	Conserve water during construction	c		

Government sustainability principles: Social progress which recognises the needs of everyone

Theme: Respect for people

Key issues	Sub-issues for Award Scheme criteria	d - design c - construction g - generic	Operational indicators (environmental and social)	d - design c - construction g - generic
Provision of effective training & appraisals	Commitment – to invest in people to achieve business goals,	g	Commitment – to invest in people to achieve business goals,	
	Planning – how skills, individuals and teams are to be developed to achieve these goals,	g	Planning – how skills, individuals and teams are to be developed to achieve these goals,	
	Taking Action – to develop and use necessary skills in a well defined and continuing programme directly tied to business objectives,	g	Taking Action – to develop and use necessary skills in a well defined and continuing programme directly tied to business objectives,	
	Evaluating – outcomes of training and development for individuals' progress towards goals, the value achieved and future needs.	g	Evaluating – outcomes of training and development for individuals' progress towards goals, the value achieved and future needs.	
	Reportable fatal and non-fatal accidents.	g	Reportable fatal and non-fatal accidents.	
Building effective channels of communication	Projects that include (and implement) a plan to consult with the end user	g		
Equitable terms & conditions	Partnership working (building long-term relationships with supply chain leaders, building long-term relationships with suppliers)	g	Percentage of part-time workers	
	Pay rates comparable with industry averages	g	Percentage of staff working with flexible hours	
	Company benefits applicable to all staff, (eg subsidised fares, private health insurance)	g	Percentage of staff offered flexible benefits	
			Percentage of staff working more than 48 hours per week	
			Number of employees opted out of the Working Time Directive	
			Percentage of employees declining offers of employment	
Provision of equal opportunities	Provision of a conducive working environment for all	g	Proportion of women employed	
			Proportion of staff from ethnic minorities	
			Proportion of staff registered disabled	
			Proportion of women in senior management positions	
Health, safety and provision of a conducive working environment	Refer to forthcoming CIRIA report *Social responsibility toolkit for construction clients*	g	See Strategic indicators for health and safety	
			Number of site employees provided with showers and rest areas in place of work	
Maintaining morale and employee satisfaction	Refer to forthcoming CIRIA report *Social responsibility toolkit for construction clients*	g	Percentage of staff involved in on-going surveys of job satisfaction	
			Percentage of staff expressing satisfaction with the way the company treats them	
Participation in decision-making	Refer to forthcoming CIRIA report *Social responsibility toolkit for construction clients*	g	Percentage of staff represented through Staff Consultative Committees	
			Percentage of eligible staff taking-up share-save or similar schemes	
			Percentage of company owned by employees	
Ensuring legal employment practices	All members of staff insured and part of National Insurance scheme	g		
Ethical investment regarding development of own organisation	Refer to forthcoming CIRIA report *Social responsibility toolkit for construction clients*	g		
Ethical investment regarding other companies	Refer to forthcoming CIRIA report *Social responsibility toolkit for construction clients*	g		

Government sustainability principles	Theme	Key issues	Sub-issues for Award Scheme criteria	d - design / c - construction / g - generic	Operational indicators (environmental and social)	d - design / c - construction / g - generic
Social progress which recognises the needs of everyone (cont)	Working with local communities	Minimising local nuisance (eg noise, vibration, dust, odour, light)	Number of formal environmental or nuisance notices served due to construction activities (affecting or arising from habitat or biodiversity, air quality emissions or dust, noise, waste disposal, spillage to water, river damage, land contamination, damage to heritage, access rights). Considerate Contractors Scheme (considerate, environmentally aware, clean, a good neighbour, respectful, safe, responsible, accountable).	g	See Strategic Indicators and Operational Environmental Indicators. Number of complaints received about inappropriate behaviour from employees working on site	
		Minimising local disruption (eg congestion)	Refer to forthcoming CIRIA report *Social responsibility toolkit for construction clients*	g		
		Building effective channels of communication	Appropriate projects that include (and implement) a plan for stakeholder dialogue.	g	See Strategic Indicators	
		Contributing to the local economy/providing local employment	Refer to forthcoming CIRIA report *Social responsibility toolkit for construction clients*	g	No indicators	
		Delivering products and services that enhance the local environment	Refer to forthcoming CIRIA report *Social responsibility toolkit for construction clients*	g		
		Education: within schools and community groups	Refer to forthcoming CIRIA report *Social responsibility toolkit for construction clients*	g		
		Social inclusion	Refer to forthcoming CIRIA report *Social responsibility toolkit for construction clients*	g		
		Involving communities in the decision making process	To what degree standards of environmental performance and social engagement have been formally agreed with the client eg. the energy efficiency of the structure (beyond minimum building standards), the need for and choice of heating and cooling systems, opportunities to use prefabricated materials or those with low embodied energy, use of secondary materials, landscaping or habitat creation opportunities, environmental performance of contractors (such as the need to have an EMS).	g		
	Partnership working	Building long-term relationships with clients	Refer to forthcoming CIRIA report *Social responsibility toolkit for construction clients*	g		
		Building long-term relationships with suppliers	Refer to forthcoming CIRIA report *Social responsibility toolkit for construction clients*	g		
		Corporate citizenship ie. resources (time/ money) spent on community/ social-ly orientated work	Refer to forthcoming CIRIA report *Social responsibility toolkit for construction clients*	g		
		Delivering buildings and structures that provide greater satisfaction, wellbeing and value to clients and users	Refer to forthcoming CIRIA report *Social responsibility toolkit for construction clients*	g		
		Contributing to sustainable development globally	Refer to forthcoming CIRIA report *Social responsibility toolkit for construction clients*	g		

Strategic Indicators

Environmental

- Percentage turnover of company operations with a formal or independently certified Environmental Management System to ISO 14001 or equivalent
- Environmental score calculated using the Business in the Environment (BiE) index of company environmental engagement
- Percentage of projects for which an environmental assessment has been undertaken and proposed environmental mitigation measures implemented
- Percentage of company sites operating under the Considerate Constructors or related scheme
- Number of formal environmental or nuisance notices served due to construction activities
- Percentage of services by value obtained from companies with a certified Environmental Management System to ISO14001 or equivalent
- Percentage of projects for which standards of environmental performance and social engagement have been formally agreed with the client
- Percentage of projects for which whole-life costs and/or Life Cycle Assessment have been calculated and used in the design of the project or in the method of construction and materials used

Social

- Percentage of staff covered under the terms of an Investors in People or similar scheme
- Percentage of annual staff turnover for permanent staff
- Percentage of services by value obtained from companies operating an Investors in People or similar scheme
- Reportable fatal and non-fatal accidents per 100,000 hours worked
- Percentage of projects that include (and implement) a plan for stakeholder dialogue
- Percentage of appropriate projects that include (and implement) a plan to consult with the end-user
- Proportion of turnover generated by projects undertaken under alliances or other forms of partnership working
- Average client satisfaction using the KPI approach

Government sustainability principles	Theme	Key Issues	Sub-issues for Award Scheme criteria	d - design c - construction g - generic
Maintenance of high and sustainable levels of economic growth, employment and profitability	Sustained & increased productivity & profitability	Maintaining and improving profitability	Profit (before tax and interest) as a percentage of sales, profit (before tax and interest) per employee. Average normalised construction cost of a project in 2003 less the normalised cost of a similar project in 2002, expressed as a percentage of the latter. Company value added per employee (£) reported in 2003 (value added is turnover less all costs subcontracted to, or supplied by, other parties).	g
		Maintaining and improving productivity	The average normalised time to construct a project in 2003 less the normalised time to construct a project in 2002, expressed as a percentage of the latter.	g
	Improved project delivery	Client satisfaction	Average client satisfaction with the finished product or facility, for projects completed in 2003, using a 1 to 10 scale.	g
		Maximising quality, minimising defects		
		Shorter and more pre-dictable completion time	Average actual duration at "commit to construct" less the estimated duration at "commit to invest", expressed as a percentage of the latter / Average actual duration at "available for use" less the estimated duration at "commit to construct", expressed as a percentage of the latter.	g / g
		Lower cost projects with with increased cost predictability	Average actual cost at "available for use" less the estimated cost at "commit to construct", expressed as a percentage of the latter / Average actual cost at "available for use" less the estimated cost at "commit to invest", expressed as a percentage of the latter.	g / g
	Monitoring & reporting performance	Company reporting		
		Benchmarking performance		
	Designing for whole life costing (life cycle)	Low maintenance and run-ning cost, product recyclability and reuse and product life expectancy	To what degree issues associated with life cycle analysis have been incorporated into the design of the product (including 'buildability', use, demolition, and subsequent reuse, recycling and disposal). / To what degree issues associated with life cycle analysis have been incorporated into the construction of the product, additional to client specifications.	d / c

Cross-theme issues, which should also be considered for an award scheme: Influence over competitors and other manufacturers, Technology transfer, Innovation, Learning

References

<www.efqm.org> (BEM, 2004)

MaSC: profiting from sustainability (BRE, 2002)

CIRIA 2001. *Sustainable construction company indicators* C563, London

CIRIA 2004. *Sustainable construction award scheme – guidance for supply chain leaders,* C619, London.

<www.constructingexcellence.org.uk/resourcecentre/kpizone/default.jsp> (Constructing Excellence, 2004)

Rethinking Construction: The Report of the Construction Task Force (DETR, 1998)

<www.fsc.org/fsc> (FSC, 2004).

<www.ftse.com/ftse4good/index.jsp> (FTSE, 2004)

<www.globalreporting.org> (GRI, 2004)

A better quality of life: a strategy for sustainable development in the UK (Office of Science and Technology, 1999)